SlideGuide

Gardner's Art Through the Ages
A Global History

FOURTEENTH EDITION

Volume II

Fred S. Kleiner

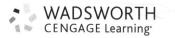
WADSWORTH
CENGAGE Learning·

Australia • Brazil • Japan • Korea • Mexico • Singapore • Spain • United Kingdom • United States

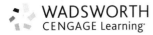
ISBN-13: 978-1-111-77187-4
ISBN-10: 1-111-77187-1

Wadsworth
20 Channel Center Street
Boston, MA 02210
USA

Cengage Learning is a leading provider of customized learning solutions with office locations around the globe, including Singapore, the United Kingdom, Australia, Mexico, Brazil, and Japan. Locate your local office at: **www.cengage.com/global**

Cengage Learning products are represented in Canada by Nelson Education, Ltd.

To learn more about Wadsworth, visit
www.cengage.com/wadsworth

Purchase any of our products at your local college store or at our preferred online store
www.cengagebrain.com

Printed in the United States of America
1 2 3 4 5 6 7 15 14 13 12 11

Contents

Chapter 14

Late Medieval Italy

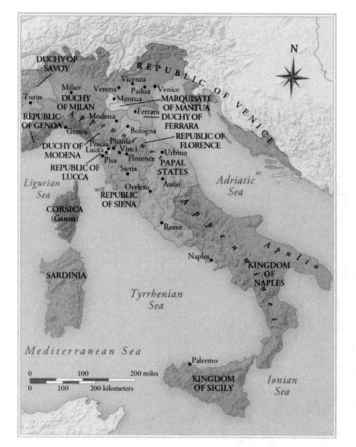

MAP 14-01 Italy around 1400.

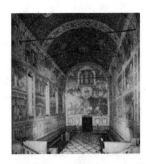

FIG. 14-01 GIOTTO DI BONDONE, Arena Chapel (Cappella Scrovegni; interior looking west), Padua, Italy, 1305–1306.

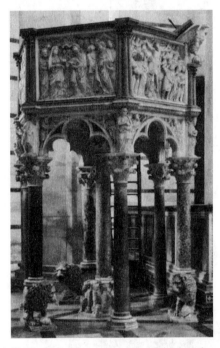

FIG. 14-02 NICOLA PISANO, pulpit of the baptistery, Pisa, Italy, 1259–1260. Marble, 15′ high.

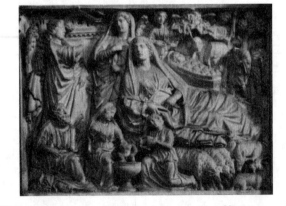

FIG. 14-03 NICOLA PISANO, *Annunciation, Nativity, and Adoration of the Shepherds,* relief panel on the baptistery pulpit, Pisa, Italy, 1259–1260. Marble 2′ 10″ × 3′ 9″.

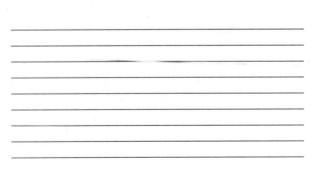

2

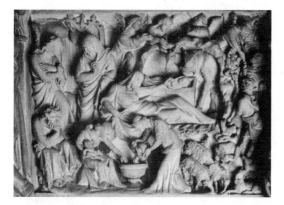

FIG. 14-04 GIOVANNI PISANO, *Annunciation, Nativity, and Adoration of the Shepherds,* relief panel on the pulpit of Sant' Andrea, Pistoia, Italy, 1297–1301. Marble, 2′ 10″ × 3′ 4″.

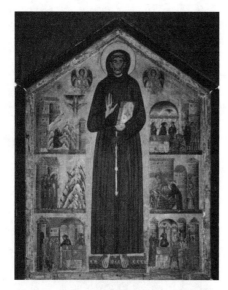

FIG. 14-05 BONAVENTURA BERLINGHIERI, the *Saint Francis Altarpiece,* San Francesco, Pescia, Italy, 1235. Tempera on wood, 5′ × 3′ × 6″.

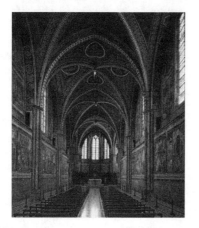

FIG. 14-05A San Francesco, Assisi, 1228–1253.

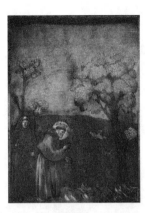

FIG. 14-05B Sr. Frences Master, *Preaching to the Birds,* CE. 1290–1300.

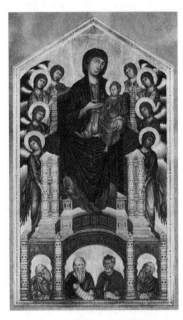

FIG. 14-06 CIMABUE, *Madonna Enthroned with Angels and Prophets,* from Santa Trinità, Florence, Italy, ca 1280–1290. Tempera and gold leaf on wood, 12′ 7″ × 7′ 4″. Galleria degli Uffizi, Florence.

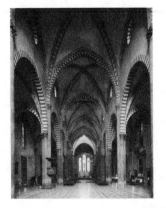

FIG. 14-06A Nave of Santa Maria Novella, Florence, begun ca. 1246.

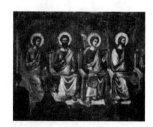

FIG. 14-06B Cavallini, Last Judgment, ca. 1290–1295.

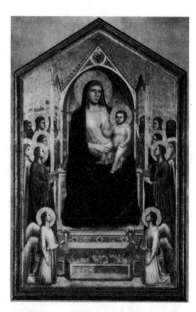

FIG. 14-07 GIOTTO DI BONDONE, *Madonna Enthroned,*
from the Church of Ognissanti, Florence, Italy, ca. 1310.
Tempera and gold leaf on wood, 10′ 8″ × 6′ 8″. Galleria
degli Uffizi, Florence.

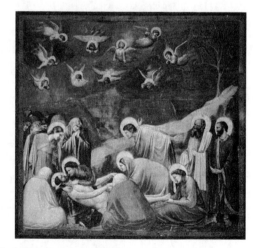

FIG. 14-08 GIOTTO DI BONDONE, *Lamentation,* Arena
Chapel (Cappela Scrovegni), Padua, Italy, ca. 1305.
Fresco, 6′ 6 3/4″ × 6′ 3/4″.

5

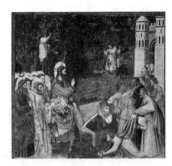

FIG. 14-08A Grotto, Entry into Jerusalem, ca. 1305.

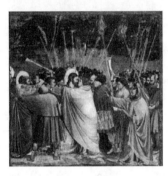

FIG. 14-08B Grotto, Betrayal of Jesus, ca. 1305.

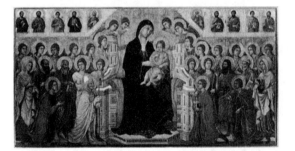

FIG. 14-09 Duccio di Buoninsegna, *Virgin and Child Enthroned with Saints,* principal panel of the *Maestà* altarpiece, from Siena Cathedral, Siena, Italy, 1308–1311. Tempera and gold leaf on wood 7′ × 13′ (center panel). Museo dell'Opera del Duomo, Siena.

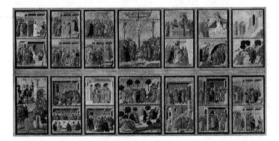

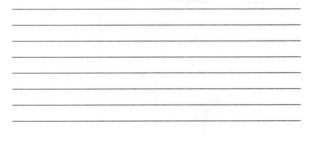

FIG. 14-10 Duccio di Buoninsegna, Life of Jesus, 14 panels from the back of the Maestà altarpiece, from Siena Cathedral, Siena, Italy, 1308–1311. Tempera and gold leaf on wood 7′ × 13′. Museo dell' Opera del Duomo, Siena.

6

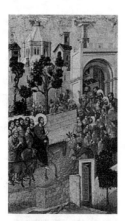

FIG. 14-10A Duccio, Entry into Jerusalem, 1306–1311.

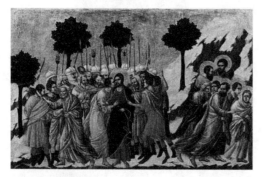

FIG. 14-11 DUCCIO DI BUONINSEGNA, *Betrayal of Jesus,* detail from the back of the *Maestà* altarpiece, from Siena Cathedral, Siena, Italy, 1309–1311. Tempera and gold leaf on wood detail 1′ 10 1/2″ × 3′ 4″. Museo dell'Opera del Duomo, Siena.

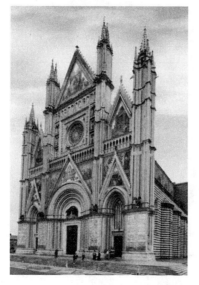

FIG. 14-12 Lorenzo Maitani, Orvieto Cathedral (looking northeast), Orvieto, Italy, begun 1310.

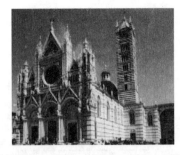

FIG. 14-12A Sienna Cathedral, begun ca. 1226.

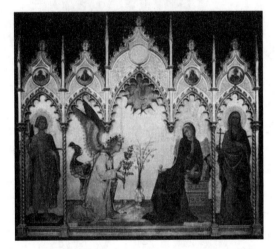

FIG. 14-13 SIMONE MARTINI and LIPPO MEMMI(?), *Annunciation* altarpiece, from Siena Cathedral, 1333 (frame reconstructed in the 19th century). Tempera and gold leaf on wood center panel 10′ 1″ × 8′ 8 3/4″. Galleria degli Uffizi, Florence.

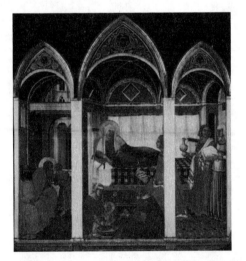

FIG. 14-14 PIETRO LORENZETTI, *Birth of the Virgin,* from the altar of Saint Savinus, Siena Cathedral, Siena, Italy, 1342. Tempera on wood, 6′ 1″ × 5′ 11″. Museo dell'Opera del Duomo, Siena.

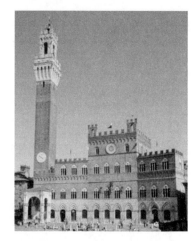

FIG. 14-15 Aerial view of the Campo (looking southeast) with the Palazzo Pubblico, Siena, Italy, 1288–1309.

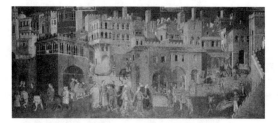

FIG. 14-16 AMBROGIO LORENZETTI, *Peaceful City,* detail *from Effects of Good Government in the City and the Country,* east wal, Sala della Pace, Palazzo Pubblico, Siena, Italy, 1338–1339. Fresco.

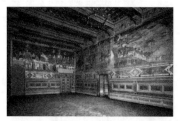

FIG. 14-16A Sala della Pace, Siena, 1338–1339.

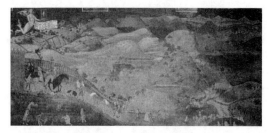

FIG. 14-17 AMBROGIO LORENZETTI, *Peaceful Country,* detail from *Effects of Good Government in the City and in the Country,* east wall, Sala della Pace (Fig.-16A), Sala della Pace, Palazzo Pubblico, Siena, Italy, 1338–1339. Fresco.

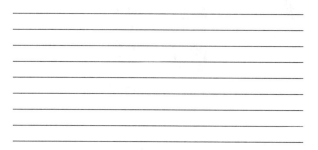

9

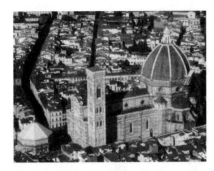

FIG. 14-18 Arnolfo Di Cambio and others, aerial view of Santa Maria del Fiore (and the Baptistery of San Giovanni; looking northeast) Florence, Italy, begun 1296. Campanile designed by Giotto di Bondone, 1334.

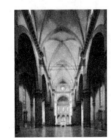

FIG. 14-18A Nave, Florence Cathedral, begun 1296.

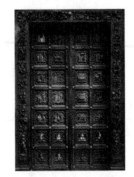

FIG. 14-18B Palazzo della Signoria, Florence, 1299–1310.

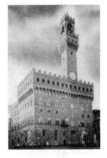

FIG. 14-19 ANDREA PISANO, south doors of the Baptistery, of San San Giovanni (Fig. 12-27) Florence, Italy, 1330–1336. Gilded bronze, doors 16′ × 9′ 2″; individual panels 1′ 7 1/4″ × 1′ 5″. (The door frames date to the mid-15th century.)

10

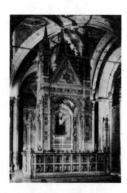

FIG. 14-19A Orcagna or San Michele tabernacle 1355–1359.

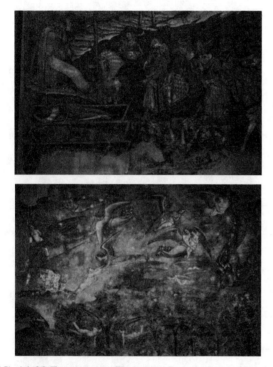

FIG. 14-20 FRANCESCO TRAINI or BUONAMICO BUFFALMACCO, two details of *Triumph of Death,* 1330s. Full fresco, 18′ 6″ × 49′ 2″. Camposanto, Pisa.

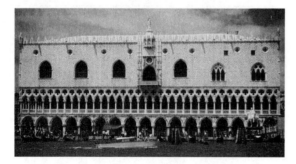

FIG. 14-21 Doge's Palace, Venice, Italy, begun ca. 1340–1345; expanded and remodeled 1424–38.

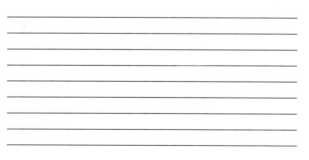

Chapter 20

Late Medieval and Early Renaissance Northern Europe

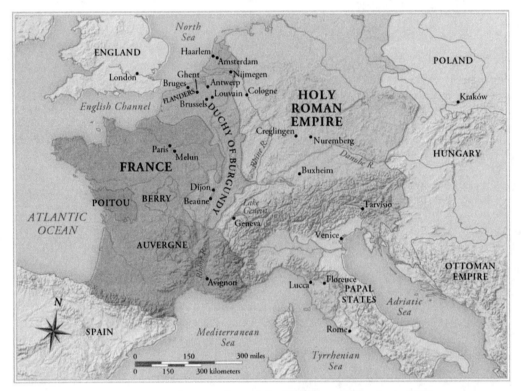

MAP 20-01 France, the duchy of Burgundy, and the Holy Roman Empire in 1477.

_____

_____

_____

_____

_____

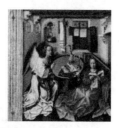

FIG. 20-01 ROBERT CAMPIN (Master of Flemalle), Merode Alterpiece (open), ca. 1425–1428. Oil on wood, center panel 2′1 3/8″ × 2′7/8, each wing 2′1 2/8 × 10 7/8″. Metropolitan Museum of Art, New York (the Closters Collection, 1956).

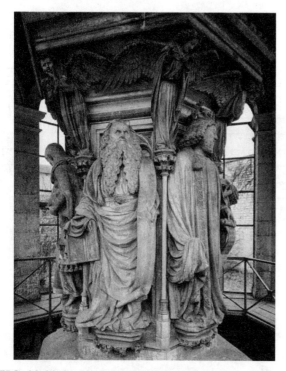

FIG. 20-02 CLAUS SLUTER, *Well of Moses,* Chartreuse de Champmol, Dijon, France, 1395–1406. Limestone with traces of paint, Moses 6′ high.

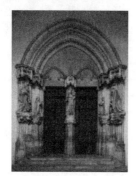

FIG. 20-02A SLUTER, Charteuse de Champmol Portal, 1385–1393.

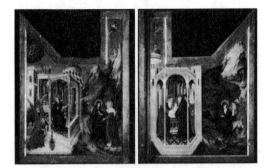

FIG. 20-03 MELCHIOR BROEDERLAM, *Retable de Champmol,* from the chapel of the Chartreuse de Champmol, Dijon, France, installed 1399. Oil on wood each wing 5′ 5 3/4″ × 4′ 1 1/4″. Musée des Beaux-Arts, Dijon.

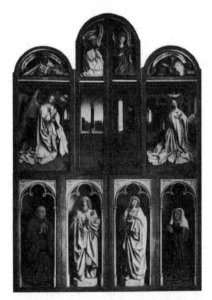

FIG. 20-04 HUBERT and JAN VAN EYCK, *Ghent Altarpiece* (closed), Saint Bavo Cathedral, Ghent, Belgium, completed 1432. Oil on wood 11′ 5″ × 7′ 6″.

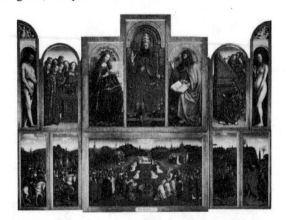

FIG 20-05 JAN VAN EYCK, *Ghent Altarpiece* (open), Saint Bavo Cathedral, Ghent, Belgium, completed 1432. Oil on wood, 11′ 5″ × 15′ 1″.

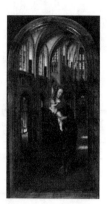

FIG 20-05A VAN EYCK, Madonna in a church, ca. 1425–1430.

_____
_____
_____
_____
_____
_____
_____
_____
_____

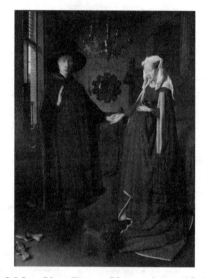

FIG. 20-06 JAN VAN EYCK, Giovanni Arnolfini and His Wife, 1434. Oil on wood, 2′9″ × 1′10 1/2″. National Gallery, London.

_____
_____
_____
_____
_____
_____
_____
_____
_____
_____
_____

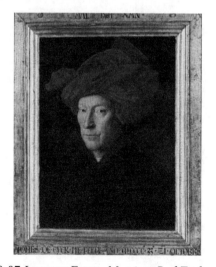

FIG. 20-07 JAN VAN EYCK, _Man in a Red Turban,_ 1433. Oil on wood, 1′ 1 1/8″ × 10 1/4″. National Gallery, London.

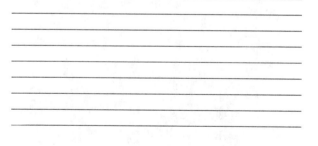

_____
_____
_____
_____
_____
_____
_____

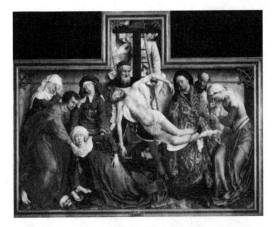

FIG. 20-08 ROGIER VAN DER WEYDEN, *Deposition,* center panel of a triptych from Notre-Dame hors-les-murs, Louvain, Belgium, ca. 1435. Oil on wood, 7′ 2 5/8″ × 8′ 7 1/8″. Museo del Prado, Madrid.

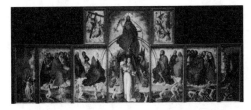

FIG. 20-08A VAN DER WEYDEN, Last Judgment Alterpiece, CA. 1444–1448.

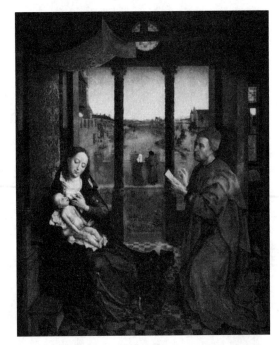

FIG. 20-09 ROGIER VAN DER WEYDEN, *Saint Luke Drawing the Virgin,* ca. 1435–1440. Oil and tempera on wood, 4′ 6 1/8″ × 3′ 7 5/8″. Museum of Fine Arts, Boxton. (Gift of Mr. and Mrs. Henry Lee Higginson).

16

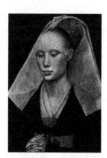

FIG. 20-09A Van Der Weyden, Portrain of a Lady, ca. 1460.

_____
_____
_____
_____
_____
_____
_____
_____
_____
_____

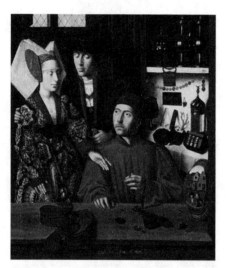

FIG. 20-10 Petrus Christus, *A Goldsmith in His Shop,* 1449. Oil on wood, 3′ 3″ × 2′ 10″. Metropolitan Museum of Art, New York (Robert Lehman Collection, 1975).

_____
_____
_____
_____
_____
_____
_____
_____
_____

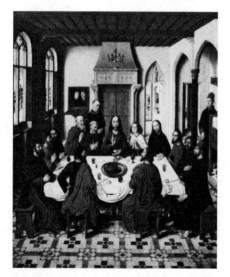

FIG. 20-11 Dirk Bouts, *Last Supper,* center panel of the *Altarpiece of the Holy Sacrament,* Saint Peter's, Louvain, Belgium, 1464–1468. Oil on wood, 6′ × 5′.

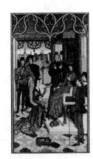

FIG. 20-11A Bouts, Justice of Otto III, ca. 1470–1475.

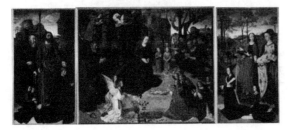

FIG. 20-12 Hugo van der Goes, *Portinari Altarpiece* (open), from Sant'Egidio, Florence, Italy, ca. 1476. Tempera and oil on wood center panel 8′ 3 1/2″ × 10′, each wing 8′ 3 1/2″ × 4′ 7 1/2″. Galleria degli Uffizi, Florence.

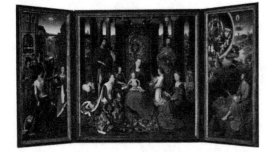

FIG. 20-13 Hans Memling, *Virgin with Saints and Angels,* center panel of the *Saint John Altarpiece,* Hospitaal Sint Jan, Bruges, Belgium, 1479. Oil on wood, 5′ 7 3/4″ × 5′ 7 3/4″ (center panel), 5′ 7 3/4″ × 2′ 7 1/8″ (each wing).

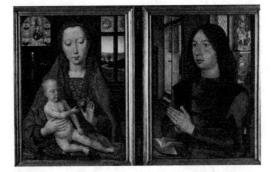

FIG. 20-14 Hans Memling, Diptych of Martin van Nieuwenhove, 1487. Oil on wood, each panel 1′ 5 3/8″ × 1′ 1″. Memlingmuseum, Bruges.

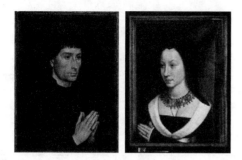

FIG. 20-14A MEMLING, Tommaso Portinari, and maria Baroncelli, ca. 1470.

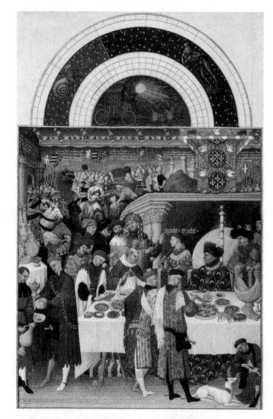

FIG. 20-15 LIMBOURG BROTHERS (POL, JEAN, HERMAN), *January,* from *Les Très Riches Heures du Duc de Berry,* 1413–1416. Ink on vellum, 8 7/8″ × 5 3/8″. Musée Condé, Chantilly.

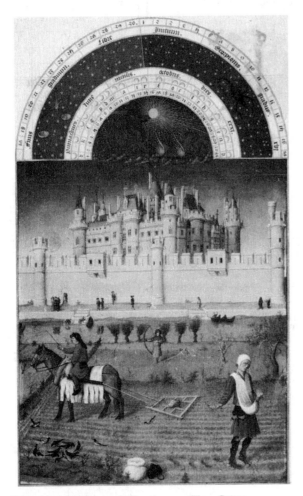

_____
_____
_____
_____
_____
_____
_____
_____
_____

FIG. 20-16 Limbourg Brothers (Pol, Jean, Herman), *October,* from *Les Très Riches Heures du Duc de Berry,* 1413–1416. Ink on vellum, 8 7/8″ × 5 3/8″. Musée Condé, Chantilly.

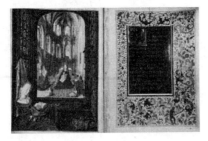

_____
_____
_____
_____
_____
_____
_____
_____

FIG. 20-16A Hours of Mary of Burgundy, ca. 1480.

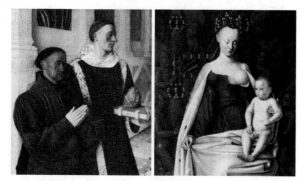

FIG. 20-17 JEAN FOUQUET, *Melun Diptych. Étienne Chevalier and Saint Stephen* (left wing), ca. 1450. Oil on wood, 3′ 1/2″ × 2′ 9 1/2″. Gemäldegalerie, Staatliche Museen, Berlin. *Virgin and Child* (right wing), ca. 1451. Oil on wood, 3′ 1 1/4″ × 2′ 9 1/2″. Koninklijk Museum voor Schone Kunsten, Antwerp.

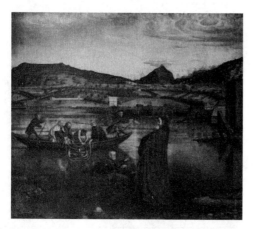

FIG. 20-18 KONRAD WITZ, Miraculous Draught of Fish, exterior wing of Alterpiece of Saint Peter, from the Chapel of Notre-Dame des Maccabees, Cathedral of Saint Peter, Geneva, Switzerland, 1444. Oil on wood, 4′3″ × 5′1″. Musee d'Art et d'Histoire, Geneva.

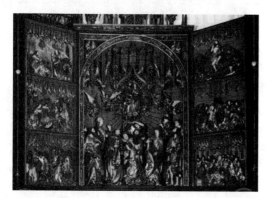

FIG. 20-19 VEIT SROSS, Death and Assumption of the Virgin (wings open), altar of the Virgin Mary, church of Saint Mary, Krakow, Poland, 1477–1489. Painted and gilded wood, center panel 23′9″ high.

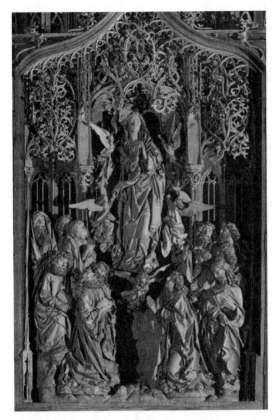

FIG. 20-20 TILMAN RIEMENSCHNEIDER, *The Assumption of the Virgin,* center panel of the *Creglingen Altarpiece,* Herrgottskirche, Creglingen, Germany, ca. 1495–1499. Lindenwood, 6′ 1″ wide.

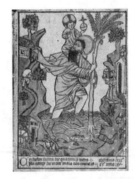

FIG. 20-20A BUXHEIM SAINT CHRISTOPHER, 1423.

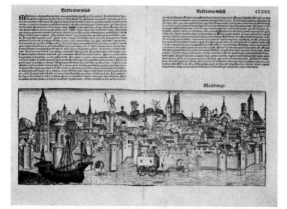

FIG. 20-21 MICHEL WOLGEMUT and shop, *Tarvisium,* page from the *Nuremberg Chronicle,* 1493. Woodcut, 1′ 2″ × 9″. Printed by Anton Koberger.

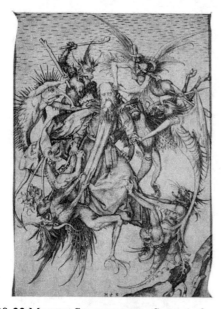

FIG. 20-22 MARTIN SCHONGAUER, *Saint Anthony Tormented by Demons,* ca. 1480–1490. Engraving, 1′ 1/4″ × 9″. Fondazione Magnani Rocca, Corte di Mamiano.

Chapter 21

The Renaissance in Quattrocento Italy

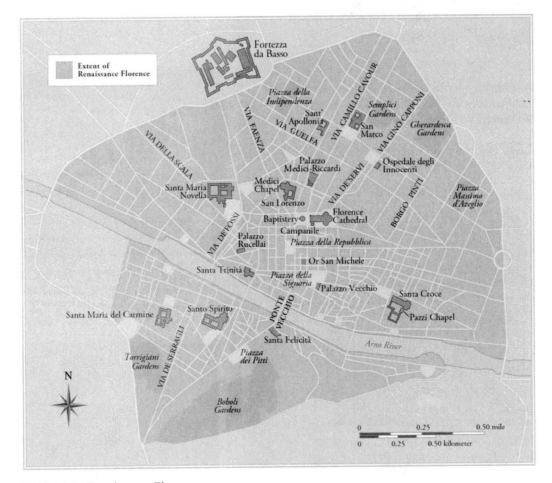

MAP 21-01 Renaissance Florence.

24

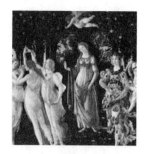

FIG. 21-01 SANDRO BOTTICELLI, Primavera, ca. 1482. Tempera on wood, 6′8″ × 10′4″. Galleria degli Uffizl, Florence.

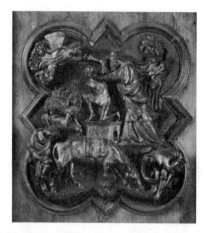

FIG. 21-02 FILIPPO BRUNELLESCHI, *Sacrifice of Isaac,* competition panel for east doors of the Baptistery of San Giovanni, Florence, Italy, 1401–1402. Gilded bronze, 1′ 9″ × 1′ 5 1/2″. Museo Nazionale del Bargello, Florence.

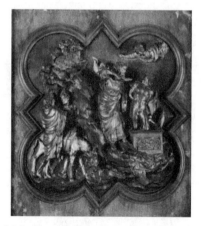

FIG. 21-03 LORENZO GHIBERTI, *Sacrifice of Isaac,* competition panel for east doors of the Baptistery of San Giovanni, Florence, Italy, 1401–1402. Gilded bronze, 1 9″ × 1′ 5 1/2″. Museo Nazionale del Bargello, Florence.

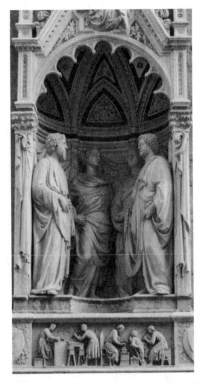

FIG. 21-04 NANNI DI BANCO, *Four Crowned Saints,*
Or San Michele, Florence, Italy, ca. 1408–1416.
Marble, figures 6′ high. Modern copy in exterior niche.
Original sculpture in museum on second floor of Or
San Michele, Florence.

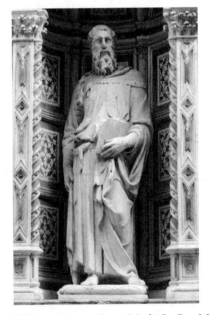

FIG. 21-05 DONATELLO, *Saint Mark,* Or San Michele,
Florence, Italy, ca. 1411–1413. Marble, 7′ 9″ high.
Modern copy in exterior niche. Original sculpture in
museum on second floor of Or San Michele, Florence.

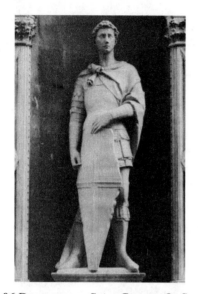

FIG. 21-06 DONATELLO, *Saint George,* Or San Michele, Florence, Italy, ca. 1410–1415. Marble, 6′ 10″ high. Museo Nazionale del Bargello, Florence.

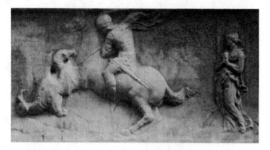

FIG. 21-07 DONATELLO, *Saint George and the Dragon,* relief below the statue of Saint George (FIG. 21-6), Or San Michele, Florence, Italy, ca. 1417. Marble, 1 3 1/4″ × 3′ 11 1/4″. Museo Nazionale del Bargello, Florence.

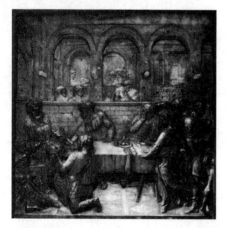

FIG. 21-08 DONATELLO, *Feast of Herod,* panel on the baptismal font of Siena Cathedral, Siena, Italy, 1423–1427. Gilded bronze, 1′ 11 1/2″ × 1′ 11 1/2″.

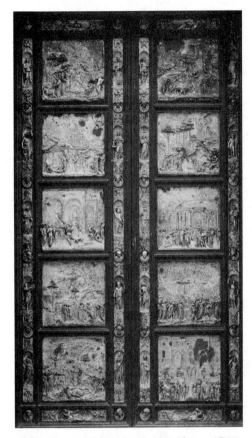

FIG. 21-09 LORENZO GHIBERTI, east doors *(Gates of Paradise),* Baptistery of San Giovanni, Florence, Italy, 1425–1452. Gilded bronze, 17′ high. Modern replica, 1990. Original panels in Museo dell'Opera del Duomo, Florence.

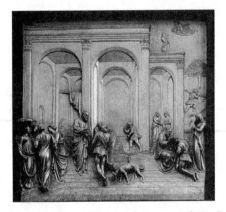

FIG. 21-10 LORENZO GHIBERTI, *Isaac and His Sons* (detail of FIG. 21-09), east doors (Gates of Paradise), Baptistery of San Giovanni, Florence, Italy, 1425–1452. Gilded bronze, 2′ 7 1/2″ × 2′ 7 1/2″. Museo dell'Opera del Duomo, Florence.

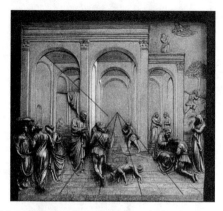

FIG. 21-11 Perspective diagram of Fig. 21-10.

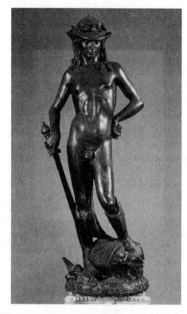

FIG. 21-12 DONATELLO, *David,* ca. 1440–1460.
Bronze, 5′ 2 1/4″ high. Museo Nazionale del Bargello,
Florence.

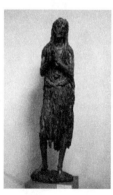

FIG. 21-12A DONATELLO, Penitent Mary Magdalene,
ca. 1455.

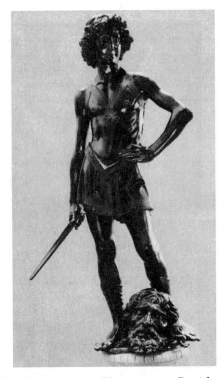

FIG. 21-13 ANFREA DEL VERROCCHIO, *David,*
ca. 1465–1470. Bronze, 4′ 1 1/2″ high.
Museo Nazionale del Bargello, Florence.

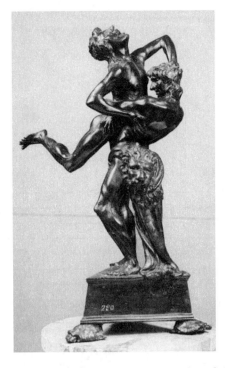

FIG. 21-14 ANTONIO DEL POLLAIUOLO, *Hercules and
Antaeus,* ca. 1470–1475. Bronze, 1′ 6″ high with base.
Museo Nazionale del Bargello, Florence.

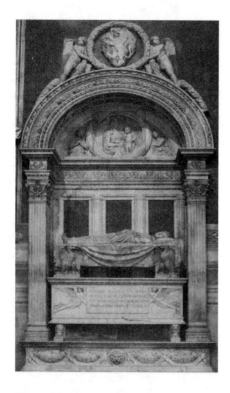

FIG. 21-15 BERNARDO ROSSELLINO, tomb of the Leonardo Bruni, Santa Croce, florence, Italy, ca. 1444–1450. marble, 23′3 1/2″ high.

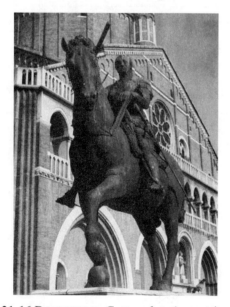

FIG. 21-16 DONATELLO, *Gattamelata* (equestrian statue of Erasmo da Narni), Piazza del Santo, Padua, Italy, ca. 1445–1453. Bronze, 12′ 2′ high.

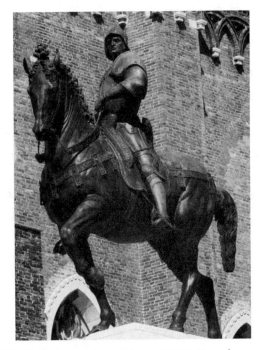

FIG. 21-17 ANDREA DEL VERROCCHIO, *Bartolommeo Colleoni* (equestrian statue), Campo dei Santi Giovanni e Paolo, Venice, Italy, ca. 1481–1496. Bronze, 13′ high.

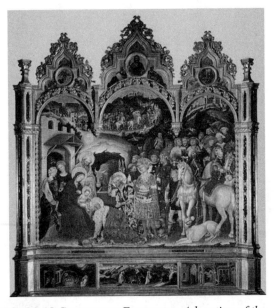

FIG. 21-18 GENTILE DA FABRIANO, *Adoration of the Magi,* altarpiece from Strozzi Chapel, Santa Trinità, Florence, Italy, 1423. Tempera on wood, 9′ 11″ × 9′ 3″. Galleria degli Uffizi, Florence.

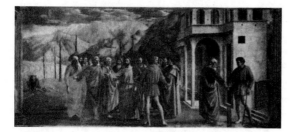

FIG. 21-19 MASACCIO, *Tribute Money,* Brancacci Chapel, Santa Maria del Carmine, Florence, Italy, ca. 1424–1427. Fresco, 8′ 4 1/8″ × 19′ 7 1/8″.

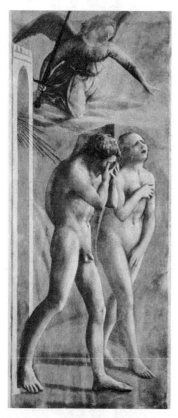

FIG. 21-20 MASACCIO, *Expulsion of Adam and Eve from Eden,* Brancacci Chapel, Santa Maria del Carmine, Florence, Italy, ca 1424–1427. Fresco, 7′ × 2′ 11″.

33

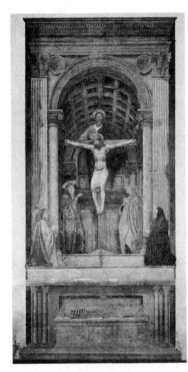

FIG. 21-21 MASACCIO, *Holy Trinity,* Santa Maria Novella, Florence, Italy, ca. 1424–1427. Fresco, 21′ 10 5/8″ × 10′ 4 3/4″.

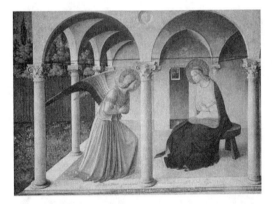

FIG. 21-22 FRA ANGELICO, *Annunciation,* San Marco, Florence, Italy, ca. 1438–1447. Fresco, 7′ 1″ × 10′ 6″.

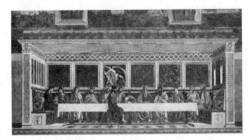

FIG. 21-23 ANDREA DEL CASTAGNO, *Last Supper,* the refectory of the monastery of Sant'Apollonia, Florence, Italy, 1447. Fresco, 15′ 5″ × 32.

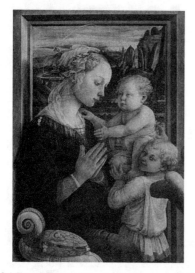

FIG. 21-24 FRA FILIPPO LIPPI, *Madonna and Child with Angels,* ca. 1460–1465. Tempera on wood, 2′ 11 1/2″ × 2′ 1″. Galleria degli Uffizi, Florence.

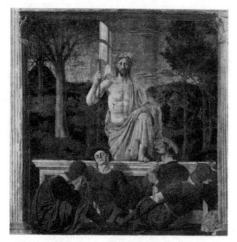

FIG. 21-25 PIERO DELLA FRANCESCA, Resurrection, Palazzo Communale, Borgo San Seplcro, Italy, ca. 1463–1465. Fresco, 7′4 5/8″ × 6′1/4″.

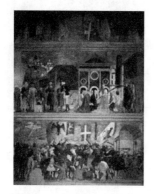

FIG. 21-25A PIERO DELLA FRANCESCA, Legend of the true Cross, ca. 1450–1445.

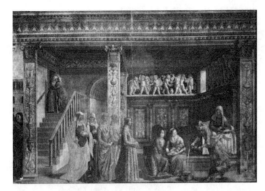

FIG. 21-26 DOMENICO GHIRLANDAIO, *Birth of the Virgin,* Cappella Maggiore, Santa Maria Novella, Florence, Italy, ca. 1485–1490. Fresco, 24′ 4″ × 14′ 9″.

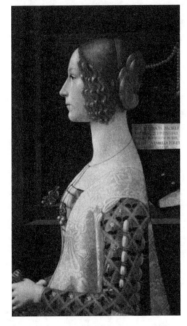

FIG. 21-27 DOMENICO GHIRLANDAIO, *Giovanna Tornabuoni(?),* 1488. Oil and tempera on wood, 2′ 6″ × 1′ 8″. Museo Thyssen-Bornemisza, Madrid.

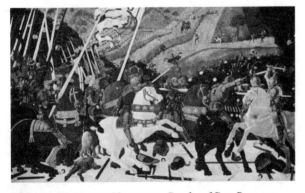

FIG. 21-28 PAOLO UCCELLO, *Battle of San Romano,* ca. 1435 or ca. 1455(?). Tempera on wood, 6′ × 10′ 5″. National Gallery, London.

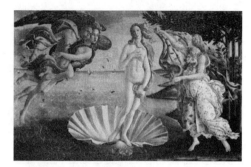

FIG. 21-29 SANDRO BOTTICELLI, *Birth of Venus*, ca. 1484–1486. Tempera on canvas, 5′ 9″ × 9′ 2″. Galleria degli Uffizi, Florence.

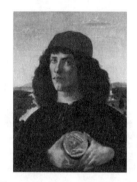

FIG. 21-29A FOTTICELLI, young Man Holding a Medal, ca. 1474–1475.

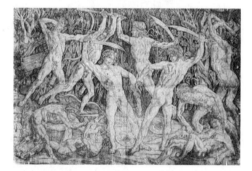

FIG. 21-30 ANTONIO DEL POLLAIUOLO, *Battle of the Ten Nudes,* ca. 1465. Engraving, 1 3 1/8″ × 1′ 11 1/4″. Metropolitan Museum of Art, New York (bequest of Joseph Pulitzer, 1917).

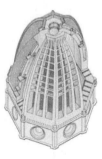

FIG. 21-30A BRUNELLESCHI, Florence Cathedral dome, 1420–1436.

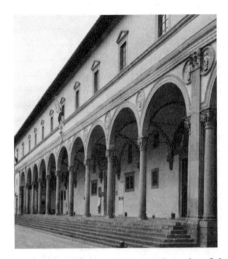

FIG. 21-31 FILIPPO BRUNELLESCHI, Loggia of the Ospedale degli Innocenti (Founding Hospital; looking northeast), Florence, Italy, begun 1419.

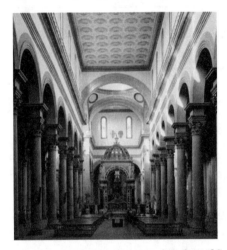

FIG. 21-32 FILIPPO BRUNELLESCHI, interior of Santo Spirito (looking northeast), Florence, Italy, designed 1434–1436; begun 1446.

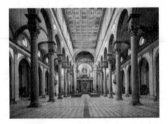

FIG. 21-32A BRUNELLISCHI, San Lorenzo, ca. 1421–1469.

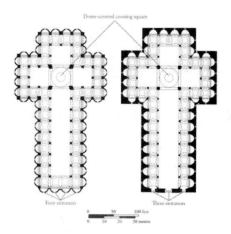

FIG. 21-33 FILIPPO BRUNELLESCHI, early plan (left) and plan as constructed (right) of Santo Spirito, Florence, Italy, designed 1434–1436; begun 1446.

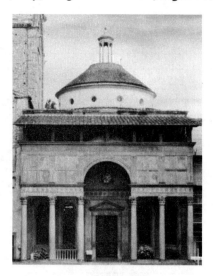

FIG. 21-34 FILIPPO BRUNELLESCHI, facade of the Pazzi Chapel, Santa Croce, Florence, Italy, begun 1433.

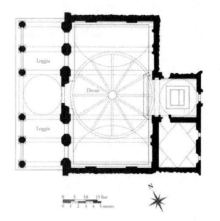

FIG. 21-35 FILIPPO BRUNELLESCHI, plan of the Pazzi Chapel, Santa Croce, Florence, Italy, begun 1433.

39

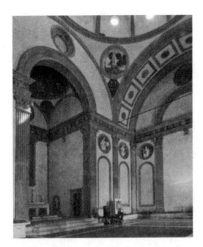

FIG. 21-36 FILIPPO BRUNELLESCHI, interior of the Pazzi Chapel (looking northeast), Santa Croce, Florence, Italy, begun 1433.

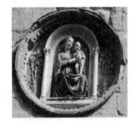

FIG. 21-36A LUCA DELLA ROBBIA, Madonna and Child, ca. 1455–1460.

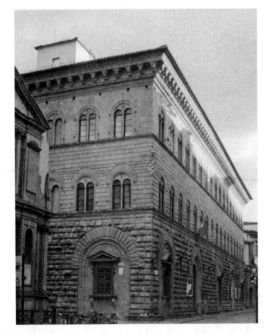

FIG. 21-37 MICHELOZZO DI BARTOLOMMEO, east facade of the Palazzo Medici-Riccardi (looking southwest) Florence, Italy, begun 1445.

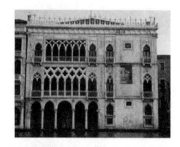

FIG. 21-37A Ca d'Oro, Venice, 1421–1437.

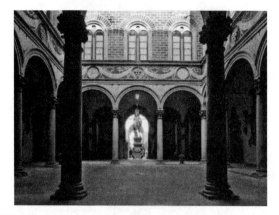

FIG. 21-38 Michelozzo di Bartolommeo, interior court of the Palazzo Medici-Riccardi, (looking northwest), Florence, Italy, begun 1445.

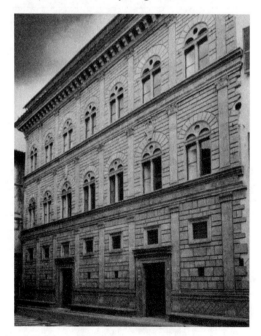

FIG. 21-39 Leon Battista Alberti and Bernardo Rossellino, Palazzo Rucellai, (looking northwest), Florence, Italy, ca. 1452–1470.

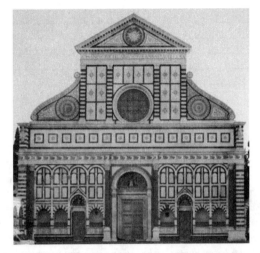

FIG. 21-40 LEON BATTISTA ALBERTI, west facade of Santa Maria Novella, Florence Italy, 1456–1470.

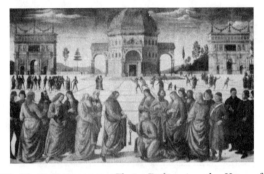

FIG. 21-41 PERUGINO, *Christ Delivering the Keys of the Kingdom to Saint Peter,* Sistine Chapel, Vatican, Rome, Italy, 1481–1483. Fresco, 11′ 5 1/2″ × 18′ 8 1/2″.

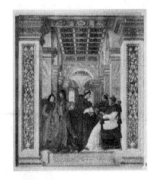

FIG. 21-41A MELOZZO DA FORLI, Sixtus IV Confirming Platina, ca. 1477–1481.

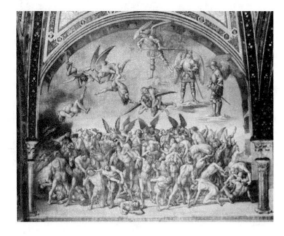

FIG. 21-42 LUCA SIGNORELLI, *The Damned Cast into Hell,* San Brizio Chapel, Orvieto Cathedral, Orvieto, Italy, 1499–1504. Fresco, 23′ wide.

_____
_____
_____
_____
_____
_____
_____
_____
_____
_____

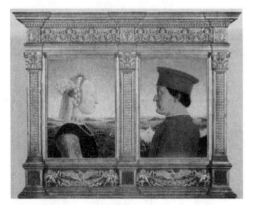

FIG. 21-43 PIERO DELLA FRANCESCA, Battista Sforza and Federico da Montefeltro, ca. 1472–1474. Oil and tempera on wood in modern frame, each panel 1 6 1/2″ × 1 1 ″. Galleria degli Uffizi, Florence.

_____
_____
_____
_____
_____
_____
_____
_____
_____
_____

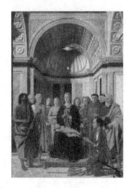

FIG. 21-43A PIERO DELLA FRANCESCO, Brera Altarpiece, ca. 1472–1474.

_____
_____
_____
_____
_____
_____
_____
_____
_____
_____

43

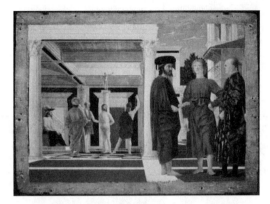

FIG. 21-44 Piero Della Francesca, *Flagellation* ca. 1455–1465. Oil and tempera on wood, 1′11 1/8″ × 2′ 8 1/4″. Galleria Nazionale delle Marche, Urbino.

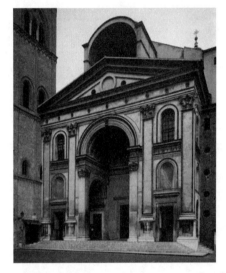

FIG. 21-45 Leon Battista Alberti, west facade of Sant'Andrea, Mantua, Italy, designed 1470, begun 1472.

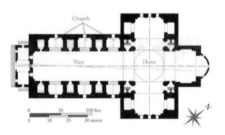

FIG. 21-46 Leon Battista Alberti, plan of Sant'Andrea, Mantua, Italy, designed 1470, begun 1472.

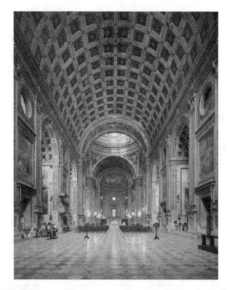

FIG. 21-47 LEON BATTISTA ALBERTI, interior of Sant'Andrea (looking northeast), Mantua, Italy, designed ca. 1470, begun 1472.

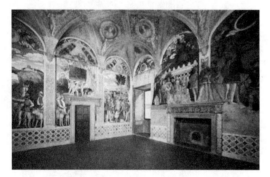

FIG. 21-48 ANDREA MANTEGNA, interior of the Camera Picta (Painted Chamber), Palazzo Ducale, Mantua, Italy, 1465–1474. Fresco.

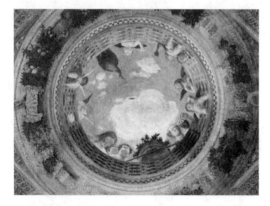

FIG. 21-49 ANDREA MANTEGNA, ceiling of the Camera Picta (Painted Chamber), Palazo Ducale, Mantua, Italy, 1465–1474. Fresco, 8′ 9″ in diameter.

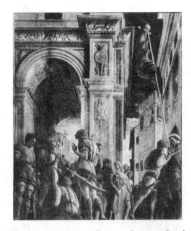

FIG. 21-49A MANTEGNA, SAINT JAMES Led to Martydom, 1454–1457.

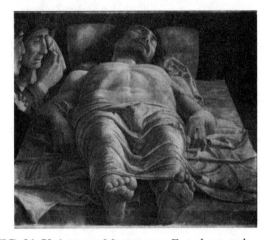

FIG. 21-50 ANDREA MANTEGNA, *Foreshortened Christ,* (Lamentation over the Dead Christ) ca. 1500. Tempera on canvas, 2′ 2 3/4″ × 2′ 7 7/8″. Pinacoteca di Brera, Milan.

Chapter 22

Renaissance and Mannerism in Cinquecento Italy

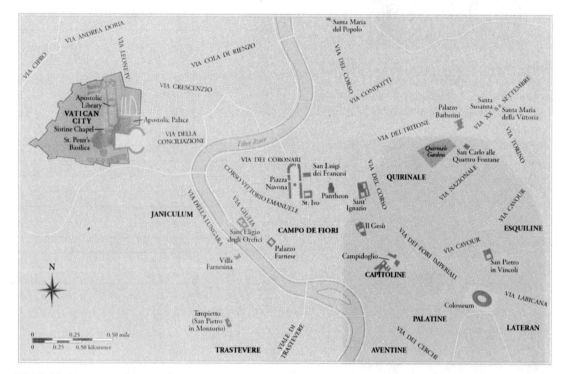

MAP 22-01 Rome with Renaissance and Baroque monuments.

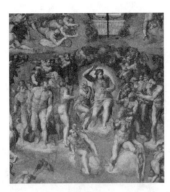

FIG. 22-01 Interior of the Sistine Chepel (looking west), Vatican City, Rome, Italy, built 1473, ceiling and altar wall frescoes by Michelangelo buonarroti, 1508–1512 and 1536–1541, respectively.

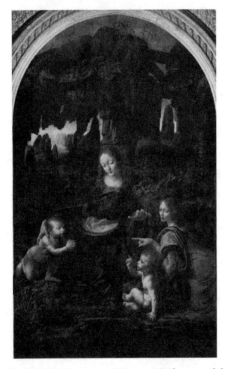

FIG. 22-02 LEONARDO DA VINCI, *Madonna of the Rocks,* from San Francesco Grande, Milan, Italy, begun 1483. Oil on wood (transferred to canvas), 6′ 6 1/2″ × 4′. Musee du Louvre, Paris.

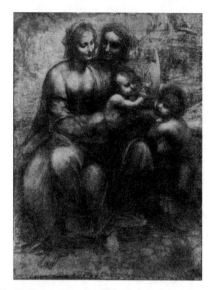

FIG. 22-03 LEONARDO DA VINCI, cartoon for
*Madonna and Child with Saint Anne and the Infant
Saint John,* ca. 1505–1507. Charcoal heightened with
white on brown paper, 4′ 6″ × 3′ 3″. National Gallery,
London.

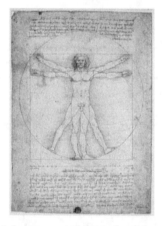

FIG. 22-03A LEONARDO, Virtruvian Man,
ca. 1485–1490.

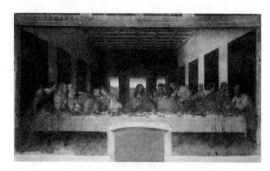

FIG. 22-04 LEONARDO DA VINCI, *Last Supper,*
ca. 1495–1498. Oil and tempera on plaster,
13′ 9″ × 29′ 10″. Refectory, Santa Maria delle Grazie,
Milan.

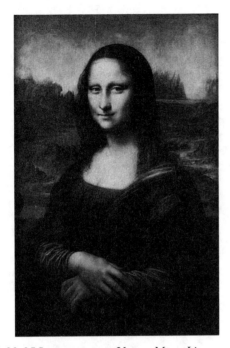

FIG. 22-05 LEONARDO DA VINCI, *Mona Lisa,*
ca. 1503–1505. Oil on wood, 2′ 6 1/4″ × 1′ 9″.
Musee du Louvre, Paris.

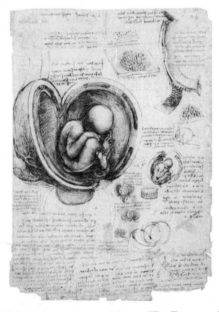

FIG. 22-06 LEONARDO DA VINCI, *The Fetus and
Lining of the Uterus,* ca. 1511–1513. Pen and ink
with wash, over red chalk and traces of black chalk
on paper, 1′ × 8 5/8″. Royal Library, Windsor Castle.

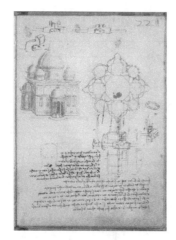

FIG. 22-06A LEONARDO, central-plac church, ca. 1487–1490.

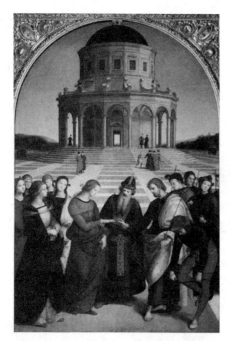

FIG. 22-07 RAPHAEL, *Marriage of the Virgin,* from the Chapel of Saint Joseph, San Francesco, Città di Castello, Italy, 1504. Oil on wood 5′ 7″ × 3′ 10 1/2″. Pinacoteca di Brera, Milan.

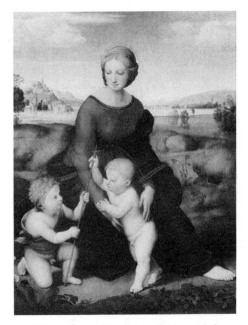

FIG. 22-08 RAPHAEL, *Madonna in the Meadow,*
1505–1506. Oil on wood, 3′ 8 1/2″ × 2′ 10 1/4″.
Kunsthistorisches Museum, Vienna.

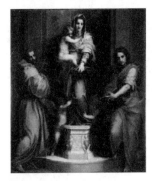

FIG. 22-08A ANDREA DEL SARTO, Madonna of the
Harpies, 1517.

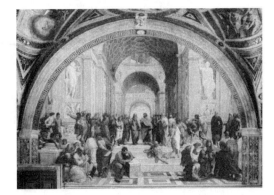

FIG. 22-09 RAPHAEL, *Philosophy (School of Athens),*
Stanza della Segnatura, Vatican Palace, Rome, Italy,
1509–1511. Fresco, 19′ × 27′.

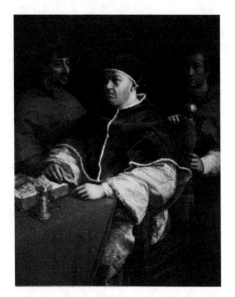

FIG. 22-10 RAPHAEL, Pope Leo X with Cardinals Giulio de' Medici and Luigi de' Rossi, ca. 1517. Oil on wood 5' 5/8" × 3' 10 7/8". Galleria degli Uffizi, Florence.

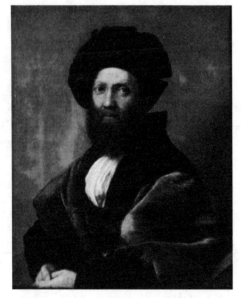

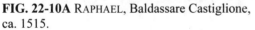

FIG. 22-10A RAPHAEL, Baldassare Castiglione, ca. 1515.

53

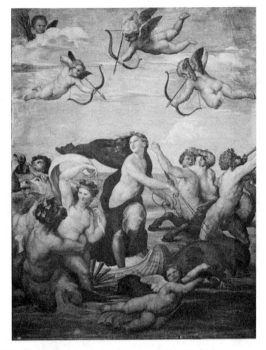

FIG. 22-11 RAPHAEL, *Galatea,* Sala di Galatea, Villa Farnesina, Rome, Italy, ca. 1513. Fresco, 9′ 8″ × 7′ 5″.

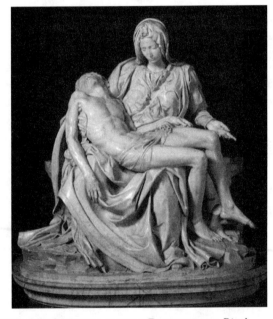

FIG. 22-12 MICHELANGELO BUONARROTI, *Pietà,* ca. 1498–1500. Marble, 5′ 8 1/2″ high. Saint Peter's, Vatican City, Rome.

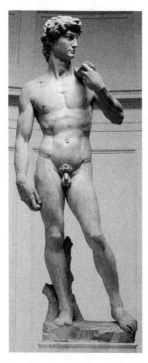

FIG. 22-13 MICHELANGELO BUONARROTI, *David,* from Piazza della Signoria, Florence, Italy, 1501–1504. Marble, 17′ high. Galleria dell'Accademia, Florence.

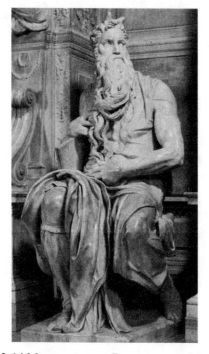

FIG. 22-14 MICHELANGELO BUONARROTI, *Moses,* from the tomb of Pope Julius II, Rome, Italy, ca. 1513–1515. Marble, 7′ 8 1/2″ high. San Pietro in Vincoli, Rome.

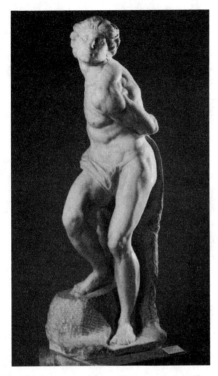

FIG. 22-15 MICHELANGELO BUONARROTI, *Bound Slave (Rebellious Captive),* from the tomb of Pope Julius II, Rome, Italy, ca. 1513–1516. Marble, 7′ 5/8″ high. Louvre, Paris.

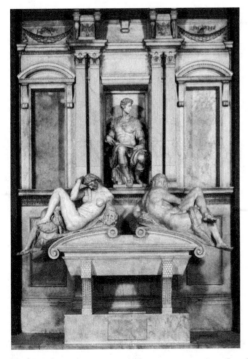

FIG. 22-16 MICHELANGELO BUONARROTI, tomb of Giuliano de' Medici, New Sacristy (Medici Chapel), San Lorenzo, Florence, Italy, 1519–1534. Marble, central figure 5′ 11″ high.

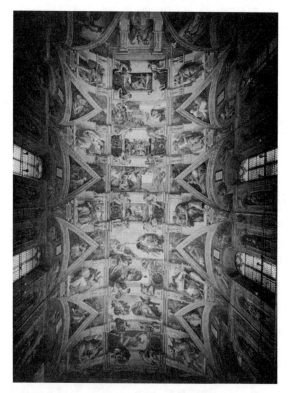

FIG. 22-17 MICHELANGELO BUONARROTI, ceiling of the Sistine Chapel, Vatican City, Rome, Italy, 1508–1512. Fresco, 128′ × 45′.

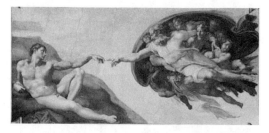

FIG. 22-18 MICHELANGELO BUONARROTI, *Creation of Adam,* detail of the ceiling of the Sistine Chapel (Fig 22-17), Vatican City, Rome, Italy, 1511–1512. Fresco, 9′ 2″ × 18′ 8″.

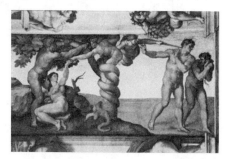

FIG. 22-18A MICHELANGELO, Fall of Man, ca. 1510.

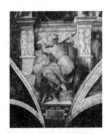

FIG. 22-18B Sistine Chapel restoration, 1977–1989.

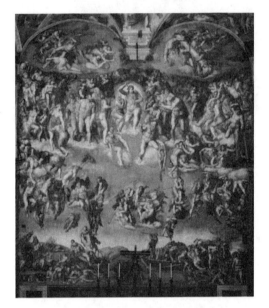

FIG. 22-19 Michelangelo Buonarroti, *Last Judgment,* altar wall of the Sistine Chapel (FIG. 22-18), Vatican City, Rome, Italy, 1536–1541. Fresco, 48′ × 44′.

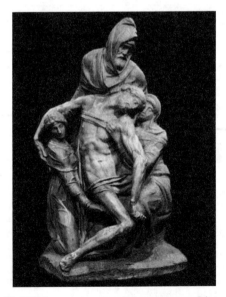

FIG. 22-20 Michelangelo Buonarroti, Pieta, ca. 1547–1555. marble, 7′8″ high. Museo dell' Opera del Duomo, Florence.

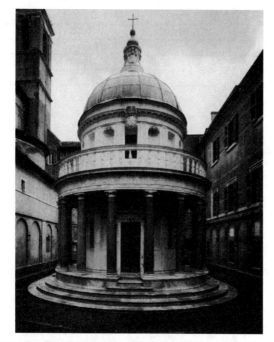

FIG. 22-21 DONATO D' ANGELO BRAMANTE, Tempietto, San Pietro in Montorio, Rome, Italy, 1502( ).

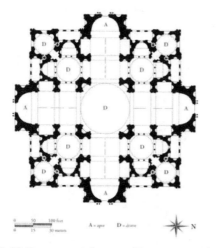

FIG. 22-22 DONATO D' ANGELO BRAMANTE, plan for Saint Peter's, the Vatican, Rome, Italy, 1505.

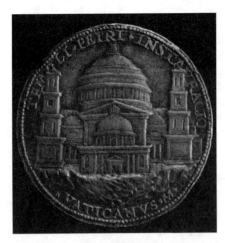

FIG. 22-23 CRISTOFORO FOPPA CARADOSSO, reverse side of a medal showing Mramante's design for saint Peter's, 1506. Bronze, 2 1/4″ diameter. British Museum, London.

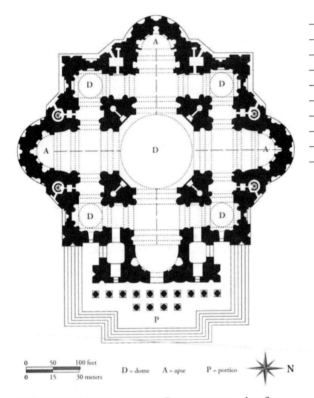

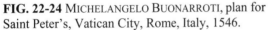

FIG. 22-24 MICHELANGELO BUONARROTI, plan for Saint Peter's, Vatican City, Rome, Italy, 1546.

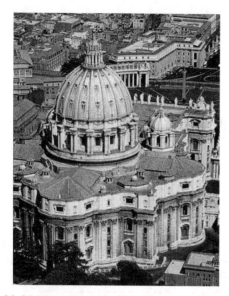

FIG. 22-25 MICHELANGELO BUONARROTI, Saint Peter's (looking northeast), Vatican City, Rome, Italy, 1546–1564. Dome completed by GIACOMO DELLA PORTA, 1590.

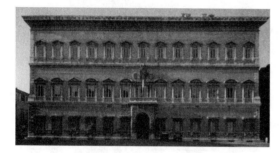

FIG. 22-26 ANTONIO DA SANGALLO THE YOUNGER, Palazzo Farnese (looking southeast), Rome, Italy, 1517–1546; completed by MICHELANGELO BUONARROTI, 1546–1550.

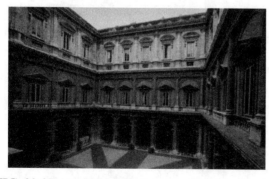

FIG. 22-27 ANTONIO DA SANGALLO THE YOUNGER, courtyard of the Palazzo Farnese, Rome, Italy, ca. 1517–1546. Third story and attic by MICHELANGELO BUONARROTI, 1546–1550.

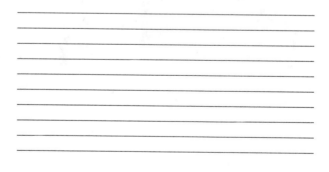

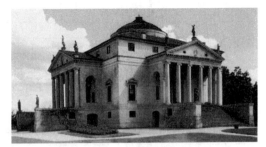

FIG. 22-28 ANDREA PALLADIO, Villa Rotonda (formerly Villa Capra looking south), near Vicenza, Italy, ca. 1550–1570.

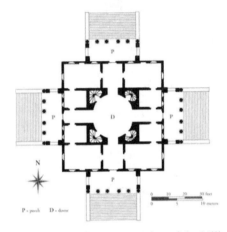

FIG. 22-29 ANDREA PALLADIO, plan of the Villa Rotonda (formerly Villa Capra), near Vicenza, Italy, ca. 1550–1570.

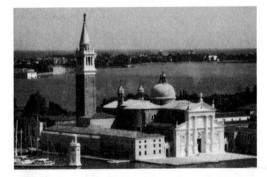

FIG. 22-30 ANDREA PALLADIO, San Giorgio Maggiore (looking southeast), Venice, Italy, begun 1566.

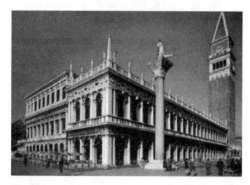

FIG. 22-30A SANSOVINO, Mint and Library, Venice, begun 1536.

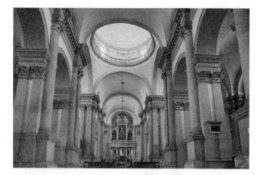

FIG. 22-31 ANDREA PALLADIO, interior of San Giorgio Maggiore, (looking east), Venice, Italy, begun 1566.

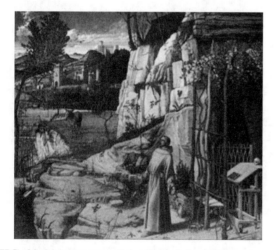

FIG. 22-31A BELLINI, Saint Francis in the Desert, ca. 1470–1480.

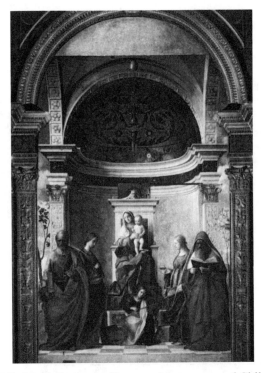

FIG. 22-32 GIOVANNI BELLINI, MADONNA and Child with Saints (San Zaccario Altarpiece) 1505. Oil on wood transferred to canvas, 16′ 5 1/2″ × 7′ 9″. San Zaccaria, Venice.

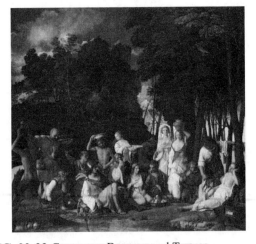

FIG. 22-33 GIOVANNI BELLINI and TITIAN, *Feast of the Gods,* from the Camerino d'Alabastro, Palazzo Ducale, Ferrara, Italy, 1529. Oil on canvas, 5′ 70 × 6′ 2″. National Gallery of Art, Washington, D.C. (Widener Collection).

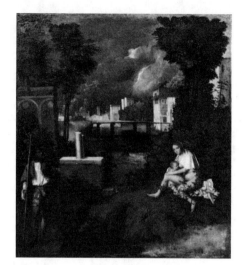

FIG. 22-34 GIORGIONE DA CASTELFRANCO, *The Tempest,* ca. 1510. Oil on canvas, 2′ 8 1/4″ × 2′ 4 3/4″. Galleria dell'Accademia, Venice.

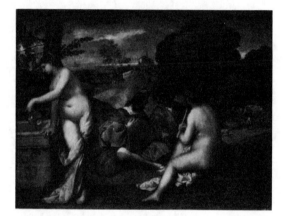

FIG. 22-35 TITIAN, *Pastoral Symphony,* ca. 1508–1510. Oil on canvas, 3′ 7 1/4″ × 4′ 6 1/4″. Louvre, Paris.

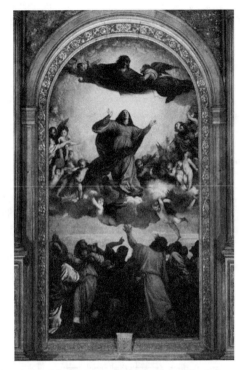

FIG. 22-36 TITIAN, *Assumption of the Virgin,*
1516–1518. Oil on wood, 22′ 7 1/2″ × 11′ 10″.
Santa Maria Gloriosa dei Frari, Venice.

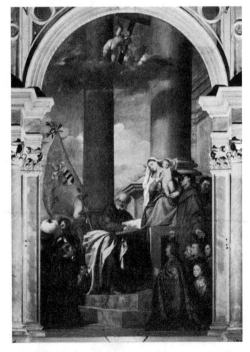

FIG. 22-37 TITIAN, *Madonna of the Pesaro
Family,* 1519–1526. Oil on canvas, 15′ 11″ × 8′ 10″.
Pesaro Chapel, Santa Maria dei Frari, Venice.

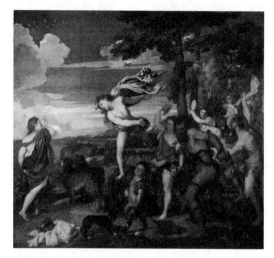

FIG. 22-38 TITIAN, *Meeting of Bacchus and Ariadne,* from the Camerino d'Alabastro, Palazzo Ducale, Ferrara, Italy, 1522–1523. Oil on canvas, 5′ 9″ × 6′ 3″. National Gallery, London.

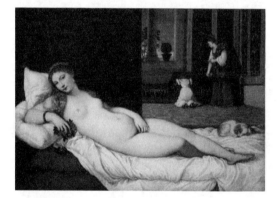

FIG. 22-39 TITIAN, *Venus of Urbino,* 1538. Oil on canvas, 3′ 11″ × 5′ 5″. Galleria degli Uffizi, Florence.

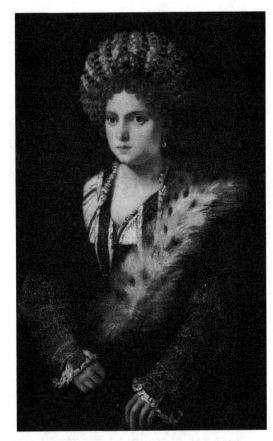

FIG. 22-40 TITIAN, *Isbella d'Este,* 1534–1536.
Oil on canvas, 3′ 4 1/8″ × 2′ 1 3/16″.
Kunsthistorisches Museum, Vienna.

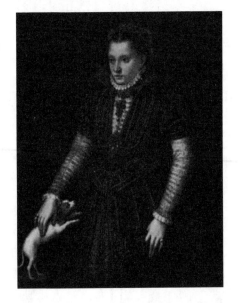

FIG. 22-40A FONTANA, Portrait of a Noblewoman,
ca 1580.

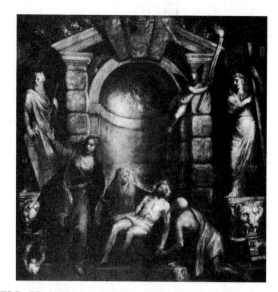

FIG. 22-41 TITIAN and PALMA il Giovane, Pieta, ca. 1570–1576. Oil on canvas, 11′6″ × 12′9″. Galleria dell Accadenia, Venice.

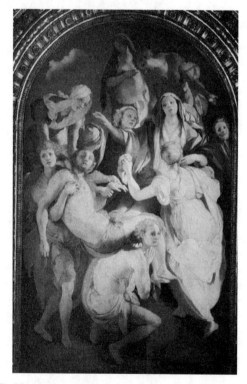

FIG. 22-42 JACOPO DA PONTORMO, *Entombment of Christ,* Capponi Chapel, Santa Felicità, Florence, Italy, 1525–1528. Oil on wood, 10′ 3″ × 6′ 4″.

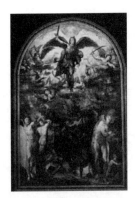

FIG. 22-42A BECCAFUMI, Fall of the Rebel Angels, ca. 1524.

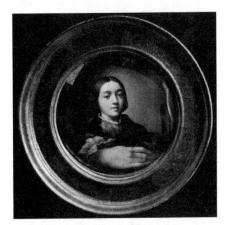

FIG. 22-43 PARMIGIANINO, Self-Portrait in a Convex Mirror, 1524. Oil on wood 9 5/8″ diameter. Kunsthistorisches Museum, Vienna.

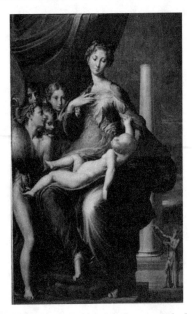

FIG. 22-44 PARAMIGININO, *Madonna with the Long Neck,* from the Baiardi Chapel, Santa Maria dei Servi, Parma, Italy, 1534–1540. Oil on wood 7′ 1″ × 4′ 4″. Galleria degli Uffizi, Florence.

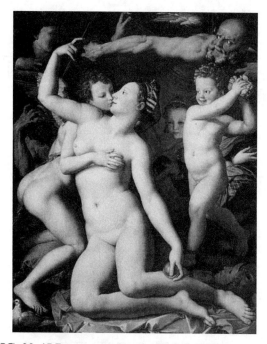

FIG. 22-45 BRONZINO, *Venus, Cupid, Folly, and Time*, ca. 1546. Oil on wood. 4′9 1/2 ″ × 3′3/4″. National Gallery, London.

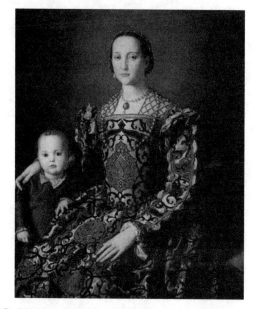

FIG. 22-46 BRONZINO, Eleanora of Toledo and Giovanni de' Medici, ca. 1546. Oil on wood, 3′ 9 1/4″ × 3′ 1 3/4″. Galleria degli Uffizi, Florence.

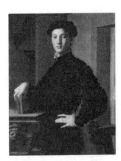

FIG. 22-46A BRONZINO, Portrait of a Young Man, ca. 1530–1545.

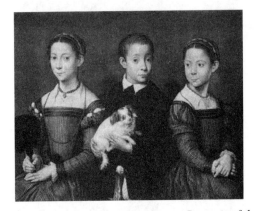

FIG. 22-47 SOFONISBA ANGUISSOLA, *Portrait of the Artist's Sisters and Brother,* ca. 1555. Oil on panel, 2′ 5 1/4″ × 3′ 1 1/2″. Methuen Collection Corsham Court, Wiltshire.

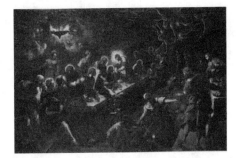

FIG. 22-48 TINTORETTO, *Last Supper,* 1594. Oil on canvas, 12′ × 18′ 8″. San Giorgio Maggiore, Venice.

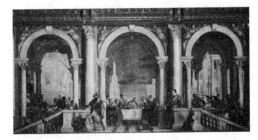

FIG. 22-49 PAOLO VERONESE, *Christ in the House of Levi,* from the refectory of Santi Giovanni e Paolo, Venice, Italy, 1573. Oil on canvas, 18′ 3″ × 42′. Galleria dell'Accademia, Venice.

72

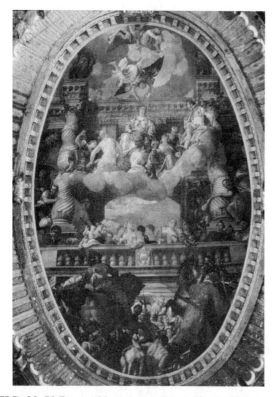

FIG. 22-50 PAOLO VERONESE, *Triumph of Venice,*
ca. 1585. Oil on canvas, 29′ 8″ × 19′. Hall of the
Grand Council, Doge's Palace, Venice.

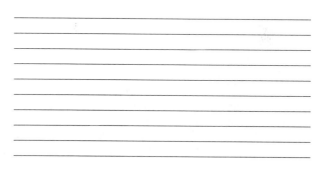

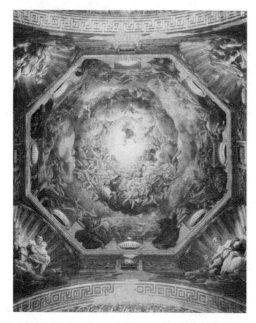

FIG. 22-51 CORREGIO, *Assumption of the Virgin,*
1526–1530. Fresco, 35′ 10″ × 37′ 11″. Parma
Cathedral, Parma.

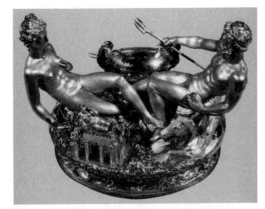

FIG. 22-52 BENVENUTO CELLINI, *Saltcellar of Francis I,* 1540–1543. Gold, enamel, and ebony, 10 1/4″ × 1′1 1/8″. Kunsthistorisches Museum, Vienna.

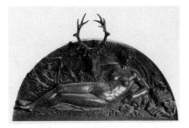

FIG. 22-52A CELLINI, Genius of Fontainebleau, 1542–1543.

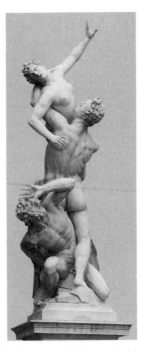

FIG. 22-53 GIOVANNI DA BOLOGNA, *Abduction of the Sabine Women,* Loggia dei Lanzi, Piazza della Signoria, Florence, Italy, 1579–1583. Marble, 13′ 5 1/2″ high.

74

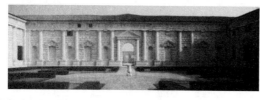

FIG. 22-54 Giulio Romano, interior courtyard facade of the Palazzo del Tè, (looking southeast) Mantua, Italy, 1525–1535.

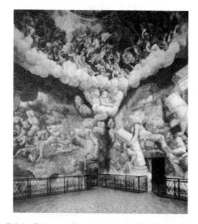

FIG. 22-54A Giulio Romano, fall of the Giants, 1530–1532.

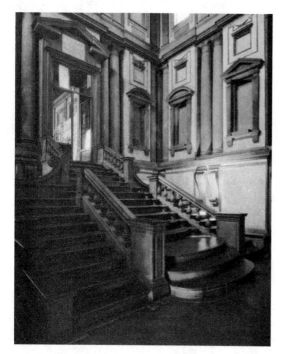

FIG. 22-55 Michelangelo Buonarroti, vestibule of the Laurentian Library, Florence, Italy, 1524–1534; staircase, 1558–1559.

75

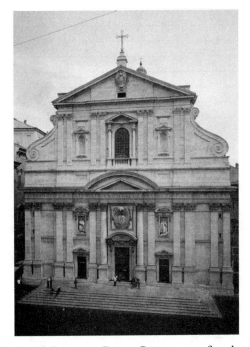

FIG. 22-56 GIACOMO DELLA PORTA, west facade
of Il Gesù, Rome, Italy, ca. 1575–1584.

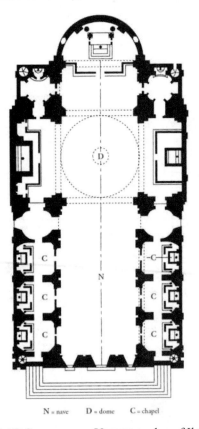

N = nave   D = dome   C = chapel

FIG. 22-57 GIACOMO DA VIGNOLA, plan of Il Gesù,
Rome, Italy, 1568.

Chapter 23

High Renaissance and Mannerism in Northern Europe and Spain

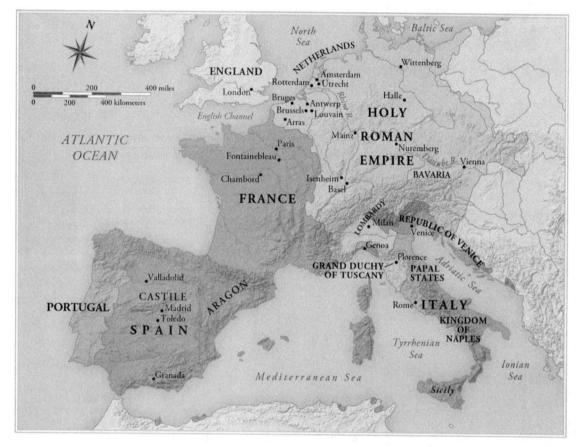

MAP 23-01 Europe in the early 16th century.

_____
_____
_____
_____
_____

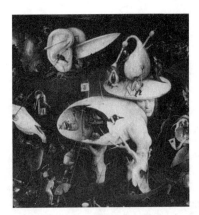

FIG. 23-01 HIERONYMUS BOSCH, Garden of earthly Delights, 1505–1510. Oil on wood center panel 7'5/8 × '4 3/4", each wing 7'2 5/8"× 3'2 1/4". Museo del Prado, Madrid.

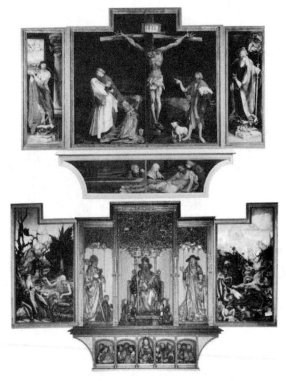

FIG. 23-02 MATTHIAS GRÜNEWALD, *Isenheim Altarpiece* (closed *top;* open, *bottom),* from the chapel of the Hospital of Saint Anthony, Isenheim, Germany, ca. 1510-1515. Oil on wood 9' 9 1/2" × 10' 9" (center panel), 8' 2 1/2" × 3' 1/2" (each wing), 2' 5 1/2" × 11' 2" (predella). Shrine carved by NIKOLAUS HAGENAUER in 1490. Painted and gilt limewood 9' 9 1/2" × 10' 9". Musée d'Unterlinden, Colmar.

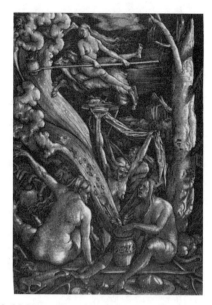

FIG. 23-03 HANS BALDUNG GRIEN, *Witches' Sabbath,* 1510. Chiaroscuro woodcut, 1 2 7/8″ × 10 1/4″. British, Museum, London.

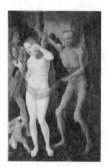

FIG. 23-03A BALDUNG GRIEN, Death and the Maiden, 1509–1511.

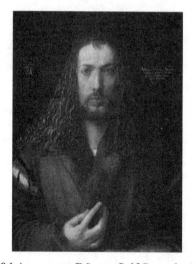

FIG. 23-04 ALBRECHT DÜRER, Self-Portrait, 1500. Oil on wood 2′ 2 1/4″ × 17 1/4″. Alte Pinakothek, Munich.

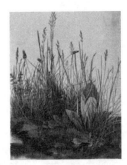

FIG. 23-04A DORER, Great Piece of Turf, 1503.

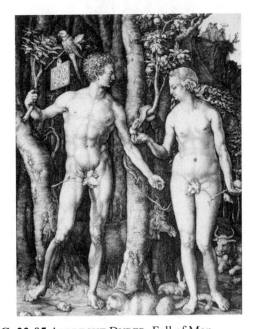

FIG. 23-05 ALBRECHT DURER, Fall of Man
(Adam and Eve), 1504. Engraving, 9 7/8″ × 7 5/8″.
Museum of Fine Arts, Boston (centennial gift of
Landon T. Clay.

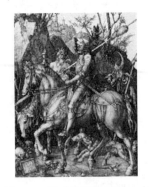

FIG. 23-05A DURER, Knight, Death, and the
Devil, 1513.

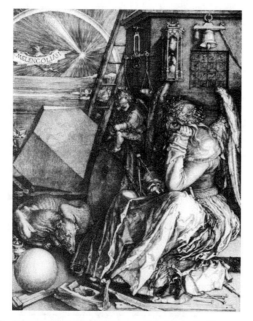

FIG. 23-06 ALBRECHT DÜRER, Melencolia I, 1514. Engraving, 9 3/8″ × 7 1/2″. Victoria & Albert Museum, London.

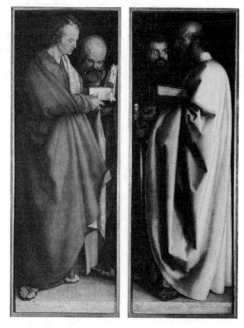

FIG. 23-07 ALBRECHT DÜRER, *Four Apostles,* 1526. Oil on wood each panel 7′ 1″ × 2′ 6″. Alte Pinakothek, Munich.

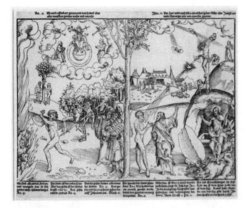

FIG. 23-08 LUCAS CRANACH THE ELDER, law and gospel ca. 1530. Woodcut, 1″ 5/8″ × 1′ 4/3″. British Museum, London.

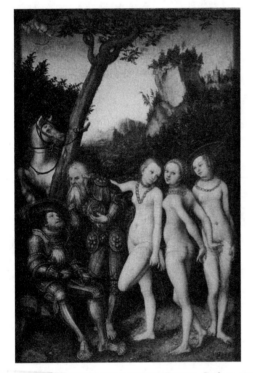

FIG. 23-09 LUCAS CRANACH THE ELDER, Judgment of Paris, 1530. Oil on wood 1′ 1 1/2″ × 9 1/2″. Staatliche Kunsthalle, Karlsruhe.

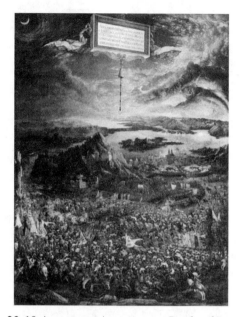

FIG. 23-10 ALBRECHT ALTDORFER, *Battle of Issus,*
1529. Oil on wood 5′ 2 1/4″ × 3′ 11 1/4″.
Alte Pinakothek, Munich.

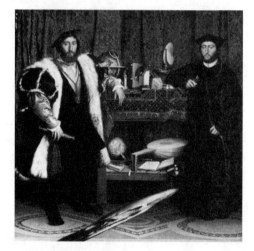

FIG. 23-11 HANS HOLBEIN THE YOUNGER, *French
Ambassadors,* 1533. Oil and tempera on wood
6′ 8″ × 6′ 9 1/2″. National Gallery, London.

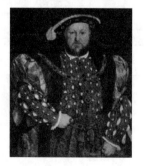

FIG. 23-11A HOLBEN the YOUNGER, Henry VIII,
1540.

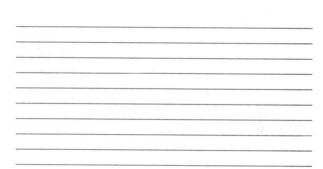

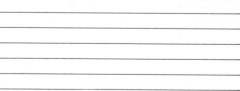

83

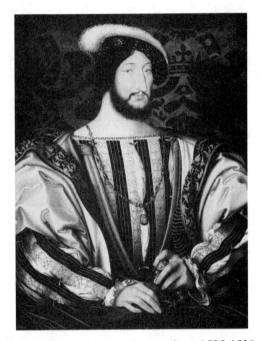

FIG. 23-12 JEAN CLOUET, *Francis I,* ca. 1525-1530. Tempera and oil on wood 3′ 2″ × 2′ 5″. Musee du Louvre, Paris.

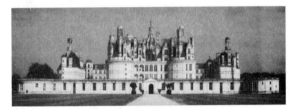

FIG. 23-13 CHÂTEAU DE CHAMBORD, (looking northwest) Chambord, France, begun 1519.

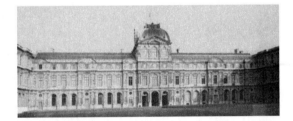

FIG. 23-14 PIERRE LESCOT, west wing of the Cour Carré (Square Court, looking west) of the Louvre, Paris, France, begun 1546.

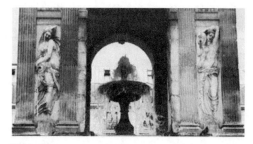

FIG. 23-14A GOUJON Fountain of the Innoncent, 1547–1549.

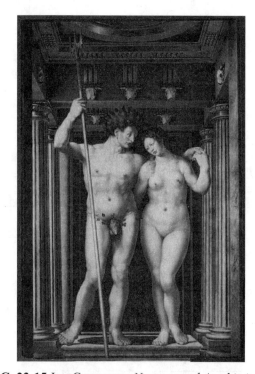

FIG. 23-15 JAN GOSSAERT, *Neptune and Amphitrite,* ca. 1516. Oil on wood 6′ 2″ × 4′ 3/4″. Gemäldegalerie, Staaliche Museen, Berlin.

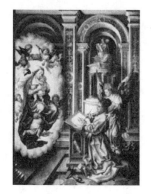

FIG. 23-15A GOSSAERT, Saint Luke Drawing the Virgin, ca. 1520–1525.

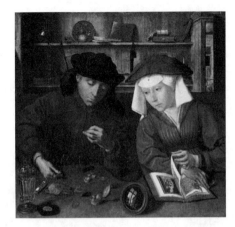

FIG. 23-16 QUINTEN MASSYS, *Money-Changer and his Wife,* 1514. Oil on wood, 2′ 3 3/4″ × 2′ 2 3/8″. Musee du Louvre, Paris.

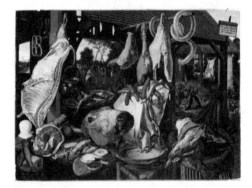

FIG. 23-17 PIETER AERTSEN, *Butcher s Stall,* 1551. Oil on wood 4′ 3/8″ × 6′ 5 3/4″. Uppsala University Art Collection, Uppsala.

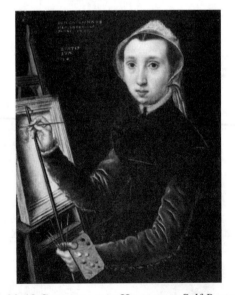

FIG. 23-18 CATERINA VAN HEMESSEN, *Self-Portrait,* 1548. Oil on wood, 1′ 3/4″ × 9 7/8″. Kunstmuseum, Basel, Basel.

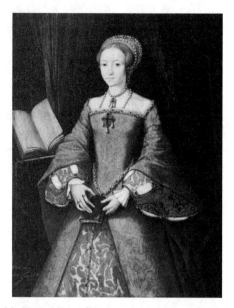

FIG. 23-19 Attributed to LEVINA TEERLINC, *Elizabeth I as a Princess,* ca. 1559. Oil on wood 3′ 6 3/4″ × 2′ 8 1/4″. The Royal Collection, Windsor Castle, Windsor.

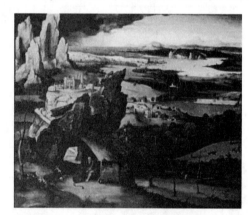

FIG. 23-20 JOACHIM PATINIR, *Landscape with Saint Jerome,* ca. 1520–1524. Oil on wood 2′ 5 1/8″ × 2′ 11 7/8″. Museo del Prado, Madrid.

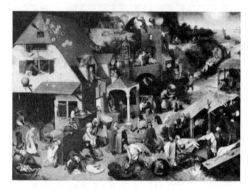

FIG. 23-21 PIETER BRUEGEL THE ELDER, *Netherlandish Proverbs,* 1559. Oil on wood 3′ 10″ × 5′ 4 1/8″. Gemäldegalerie, Staatliche Museen, zu Berlin.

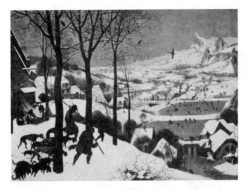

FIG. 23-22 Pieter Bruegel the Elder, *Hunters in the Snow,* 1565. Oil on Wood 3′ 10 1/8″ × 5′ 3 3/4″. Kunsthistorisches Museum, Vienna.

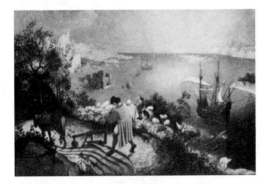

FIG. 23-22A B Ruegel the Elder, Fall of Icarus, ca. 1555–155.

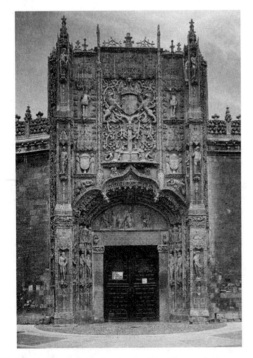

FIG. 23-23 Portal, Colegio de San Gregorio, Valladolid Spain, ca. 1498.

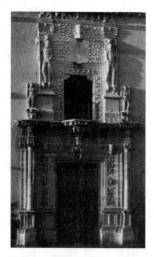

FIG. 23-23A Casa de Montejo, Merida, 1549.

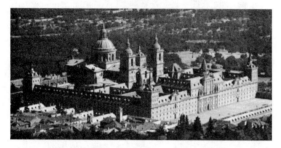

FIG. 23-24 JUAN DE HERRERA and JUAN BAUTISTA DE TOLEDO, aerial view (looking southeast) of El Escorial, near Madrid Spain, 1563–1584.

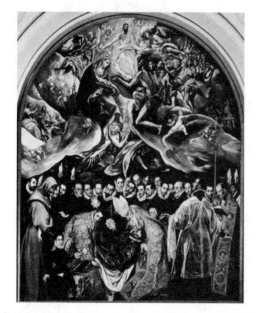

FIG. 23-25 EL GRECO, *Burial of Count Orgaz,* 1586. Oil on canvas, 16′ × 12′. Santo Tomé, Toledo.

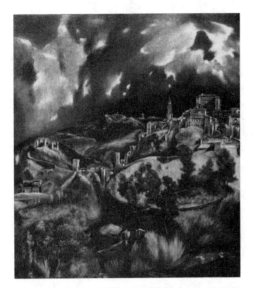

FIG. 23-26 EL GRECO, View of Toledo, ca. 1610.
Oil on canvas, 3′ 11 3/4″ × 3′ 6 3/4″. Metropolitan
Museum of Art, New York (H.O Havemeyer
Collection. Bequest of Mrs. H.O. Havemeyer, 1929).

Chapter 24

The Baroque in Italy and Spain

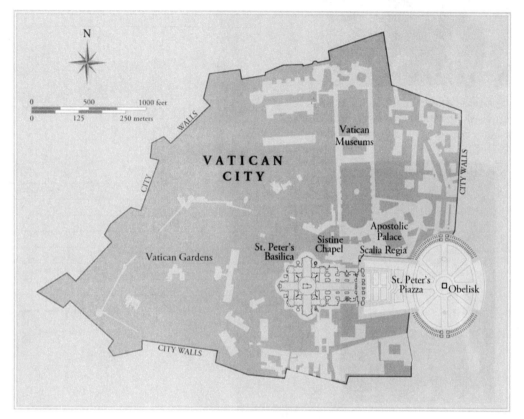

MAP 24-01 Vatican City.

_____

_____

_____

_____

_____

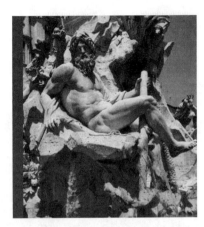

FIG. 24-01 GIANI ORENZO BERNINI, Fountain of the Four Rivers (looking southwewst with Sant' Agnese in Agonte in the background), Piazza Navona, Rome, Italy, 1648–1651.

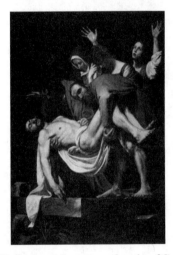

FIG. 24-02 CARLO MADERNO, facade of Santa Susanna, Rome, (looking north) Italy, 1597–1603.

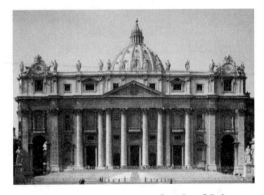

FIG. 24-03 CARLO MADERNO, facade of Saint Peter's, Vatican City, Rome, Italy, 1606–1612.

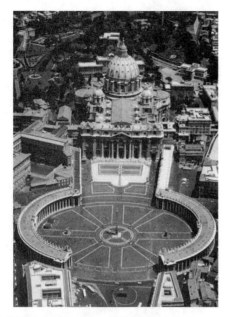

FIG. 24-04 Aerial view of Saint Peter's, (looking west), Vatican City, Rome, Italy. Piazza designed by GIANLORENZO BERNINI, 1656–1667.

_____
_____
_____
_____
_____
_____
_____
_____
_____

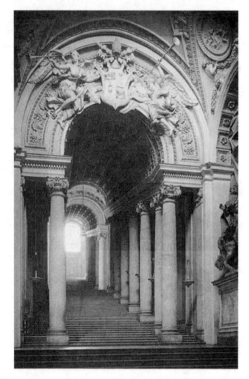

FIG. 24-04A BERNINI, Scala Regia, Vatican, 1663–1666.

_____
_____
_____
_____
_____
_____
_____
_____
_____

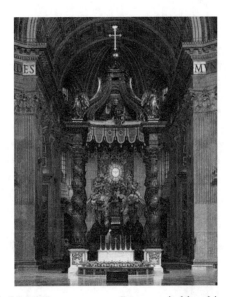

FIG. 24-05 GIANLORENZO BERNINI, baldacchino, (looking west), Saint Peter's, Vatican City, Rome, Italy, 1624–1633.

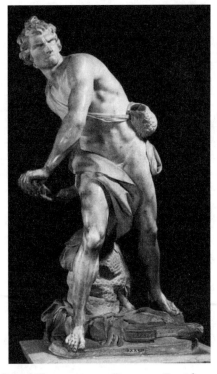

FIG. 24-06 GIANLORENZO BERNINI, *David,* 1623. Marble, 5′ 7″ high. Galleria Borghese, Rome.

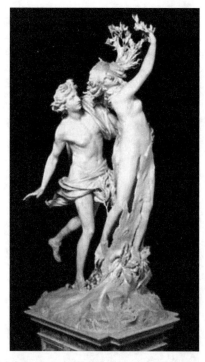

FIG. 24-06A BERNINI, Apollo and Daphne, 1623–1624.

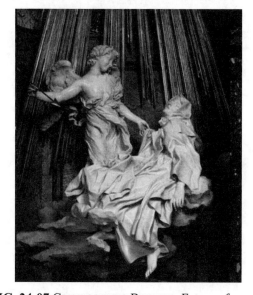

FIG. 24-07 GIANLORENZO BERNINI, *Estasy of Saint Teresa,* Cornaro Chapel, Santa Maria della Vittoria, Rome, Italy, 1645–1652. Marble, height of group 11′ 6″.

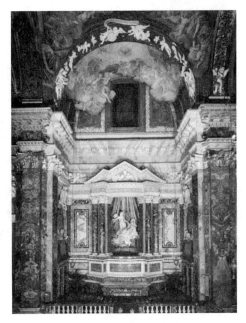

FIG. 24-08 GIANLORENZO BERNINI, Cornaro chapel, Santa Maria della Vittoria, Rome, italy, 145–1652.

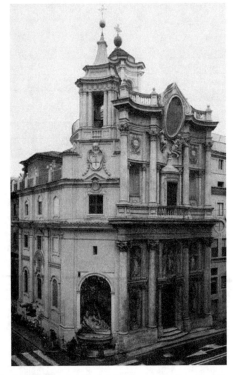

FIG. 24-09 FRANCESCO BORROMINI, facade of San Carlo alle Quattro Fontane, (looking south), Rome, Italy, 1638–1641.

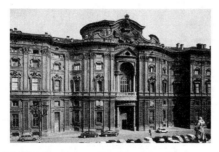

FIG. 24-09A PALAZZO CARIGNANO, Turin, 1679–1692.

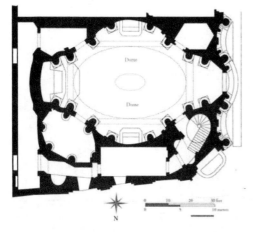

FIG. 24-10 FRANCESCO BORROMINI, plan of San Carlo alle Quattro Fontane, Rome, Italy, 1638–1641.

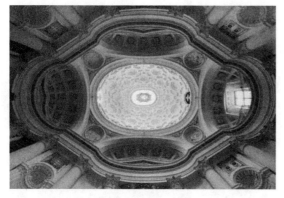

FIG. 24-11 FRANCESCO BORROMINI, San Carlo alle Quattro Fontane (view into dome), Rome, Italy, 1638–1641.

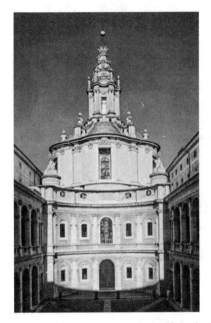

FIG. 24-12 FRANCESCO BORROMINI, Chapel of
Saint Ivo, (looking east) College of the Sapienza,
Rome, Italy, begun 1642.

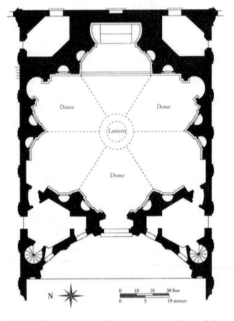

FIG. 24-13 FRANCESCO BORROMINI, plan of the
Chapel of Saint Ivo, College of the Sapienza, Rome,
Italy, begun 1642.

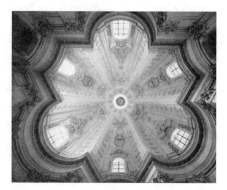

FIG. 24-14 Francesco Borromini, Chapel of Saint Ivo (view into dome), College of the Sapienza, Rome, Italy, begun 1642.

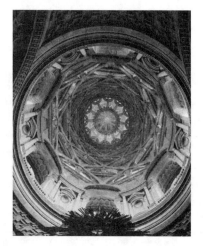

FIG. 24-14A Guarini Chapel of the Holy Shroud, Turin, 1667–1694.

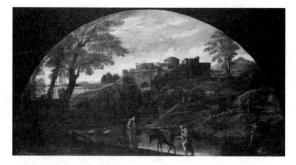

FIG. 24-15 Annibale Carracci, *Flight into Egypt,* 1603–1604. Oil on canvas, 4′ × 7′ 6″. Galleria Doria Pamphili, Rome.

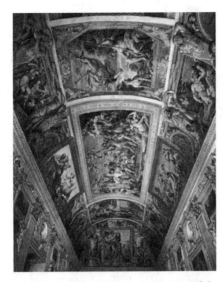

FIG. 24-16 ANNIBALE CARRACCI, *Loves of the Gods,* ceiling frescoes in the gallery, Palazzo Farnese, Rome, Italy, 1597–1601.

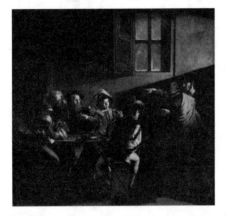

FIG. 24-17 CARAVAGGIO, *Calling of Saint Matthew,* ca. 1597–1601. Oil on canvas, 11′ 1″ × 11′ 5″. Contarelli Chapel, San Luigi dei Francesi, Rome.

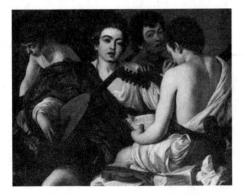

FIG. 24-17A CARAVAGGIO, Musicians, ca. 1595.

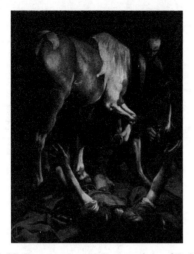

FIG. 24-18 CARAVAGGIO, Conversion of Saint Paul, ca. 1601. Oil on canvas, 7′6″ × 5′9″. Cerasi chapel, Santa Maria del Popolo, Rome.

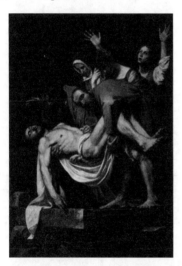

FIG. 24-18A CARAVAGGIO, Entombment, ca. 1603.

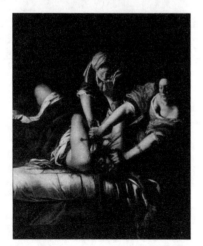

FIG. 24-19 ARTEMISIA GENTILESCHI, *Judith Slaying Holofernes,* ca. 1614–1620. Oil on canvas, 6′ 6 1/3″ × 5′ 4″. Galleria degli Uffizi, Florence.

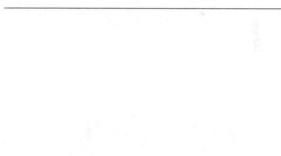

101

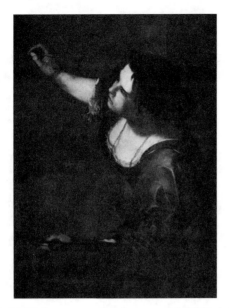

FIG. 24-20 ARTEMISIA GENTILESCHI, Self-Portrait as the Allegory of Painting, ca. 1638–1639. Oil on canvas, 3′ 2 7/8″ × 2′ 5 5/8″. Royal Collection, Kensington Palace, London.

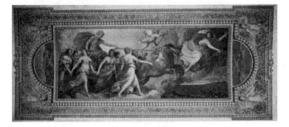

FIG. 24-21 GUIDO RENI, *Aurora,* ceiling fresco in the Casino Rospigliosi, Rome, Italy, 1613–1614.

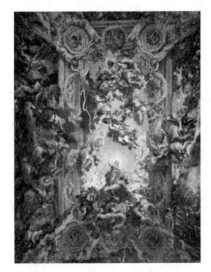

FIG. 24-22 PIETRO DA CORTONA, *Triumph of the Barberini,* ceiling fresco in the Gran Salone, Palazzo Barberini, Rome, Italy, 1633–1639.

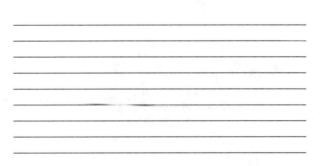

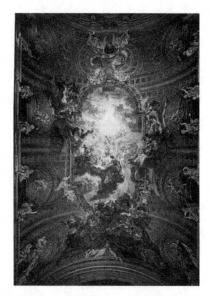

FIG. 24-23 GIOVANNI BATTISTA GAULLI, *Triumph of the Name of Jesus,* ceiling fresco with stucco figures on the nave vault of Il Gesù, (Fig. 22-56) Rome, Italy, 1676–1679.

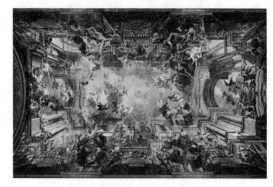

FIG. 24-24 FRA ANDREA POZZO, *Glorification of Saint Ignatius,* ceiling fresco in the nave of Sant'Ignazio, Rome, Italy, 1691–1694.

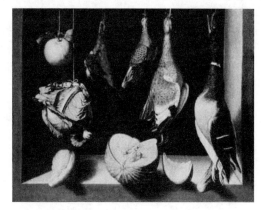

FIG. 24-25 JUAN SANCHEZ COTAN. Still Life with Game Fowl, ca. 1600–1603. Oil on canvas, 2′2 3/4″ × 2′10 7/8″. Art Institute of Chicago, Chicago (gift of Mr. and Mrs. Leigh B. Block)

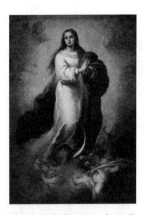

FIG. 24-25A MURILLO, Immaculate Conception, ca. 1661–1670.

_____
_____
_____
_____
_____
_____
_____
_____
_____
_____

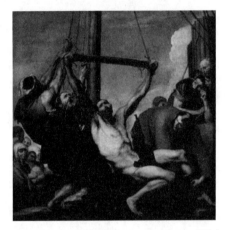

FIG. 24-26 JOSE DE RIBERA, martyrdom of Saint Philip, ca. 139. Oil on canvas, 7′8″ × 7′8″. Museao del Prado, Madrid.

_____
_____
_____
_____
_____
_____
_____
_____
_____
_____
_____

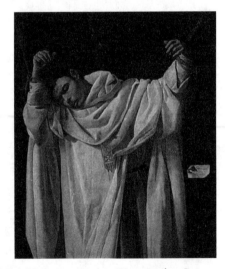

FIG. 24-27 FRANCISCO DE ZURBARÁN, _Saint Serapion,_ 1628. Oil on canvas, 3′ 11 1/2″ × 3′ 4 3/4″. Wadsworth Atheneum, Hartford (The Ella Gallup Sumner and Mary Catlin Sumner Collection Fund).

_____
_____
_____
_____
_____
_____
_____
_____
_____
_____

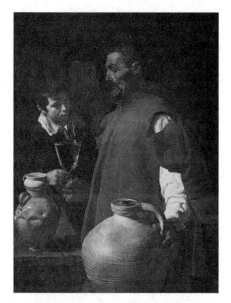

FIG. 24-28 Diego Velázquez, *Water Carrier of Seville,* ca. 1619. Oil on canvas, 3′ 5 1/2″ × 2 7 1/2″. Victoria & Albert Museum, London.

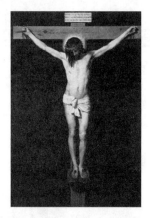

FIG. 24-28A Velazques, Christ on the Cross, ca. 1631–1632.

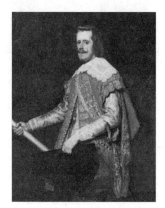

FIG. 24-28B Velazquez, Philip IV, 1644.

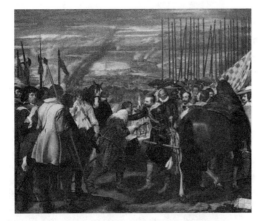

FIG. 24-29 DIEGO VELÁZQUEZ, *Surrender of Breda,* 1634–1635. Oil on canvas, 10′ 1″ × 12′ 1/2″. Museo del Prado, Madrid.

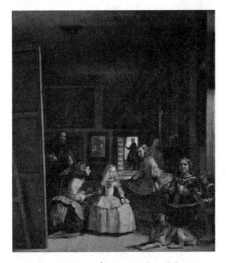

FIG. 24-30 DIEGO VELÁZQUEZ, *Las Meninas (The Maids of Honor),* 1656. Oil on canvas, 10′ 5″ × 9′. Museo del Prado, Madrid.

Chapter 25

The Baroque in Northern Europe

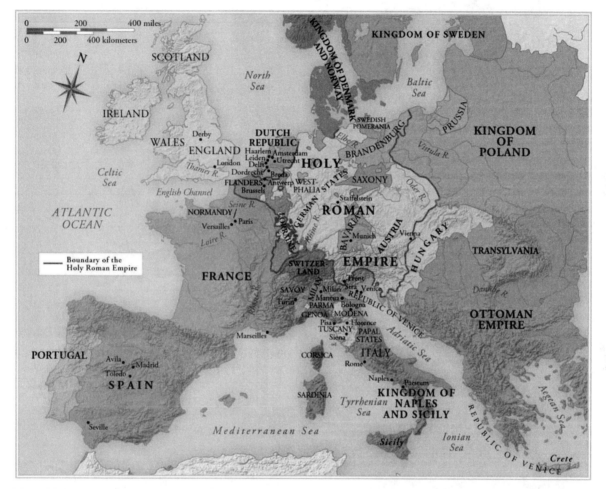

MAP 25-01 Europe in 1648 after the Treaty of Westphalia.

_____

_____

_____

_____

_____

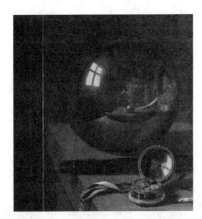

FIG. 25-01 PIETER CLAESZ, Vanitas Still LIfe, 1630s. Oil on panel, 1′2″ × 1′11 1/2″. Germanisches nationalmuseum, Nuremberg

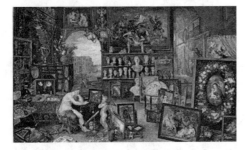

FIG. 25-01A BRUEGEL and RUBENS, Alelegory of Sight, ca. 16–17–1618.

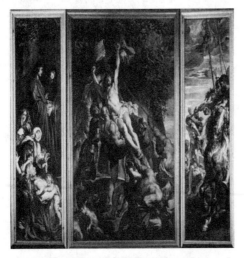

FIG. 25-02 PETER PAUL RUBENS, *Elevation of the Cross,* from Saint Walburga, Antwerp, 1610. Oil on wood, center panel 15′ 1 7/8″ × 11′ 1 1/2″ 15′ 1 7/8″ × 4′ 11″ (each wing). Antwerp Cathedral, Antwerp.

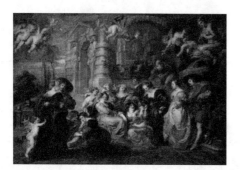

FIG. 25-02A RUBENS, Garden of Love, 1630–1632.

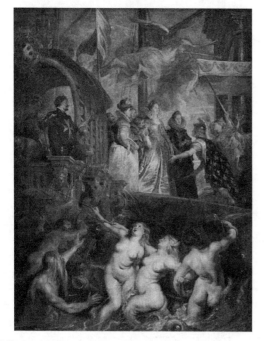

FIG. 25-03 PETER PAUL RUBENS, *Arrival of Marie de'
Medici at Marseilles,* 1622–1625. Oil on canvas,
12′ 11 1/2″ × 9′ 7″. Musee du Louvre, Paris.

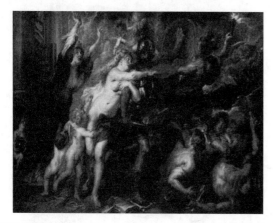

FIG. 25-04 PETER PAUL RUBENS, *Consequences of
War,* 1638–1639. Oil on canvas, 6′ 9″ × 11′ 3 7/8″.
Palazzo Pitti, Florence.

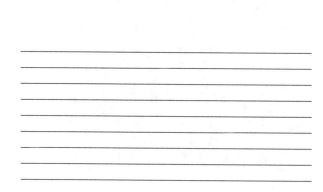

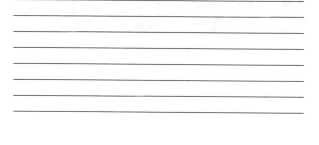

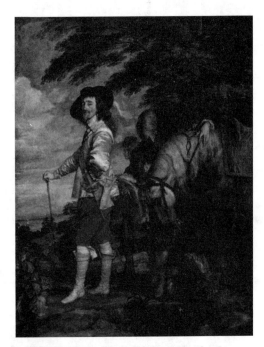

FIG. 25-05 ANTHONY VAN DYCK, *Charles I Dismounted,* ca. 1635. Oil on canvas, 8′ 11″ × 6′ 11 1/2″. Musee, du Louvre, Paris.

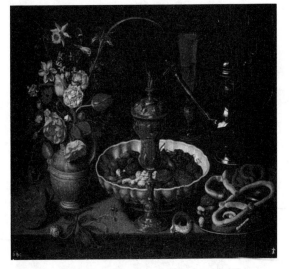

FIG. 25-06 CLARA PEETERS, *Still Life with Flowers, Goblet, Dried Fruit, and Pretzels,* 1611. Oil on panel 1′ 7 3/4″ × 2′ 1 1/4″. Museo del Prado, Madrid.

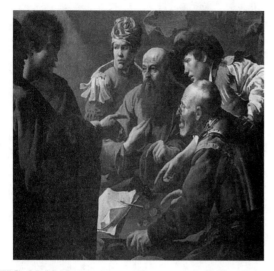

FIG. 25-07 HENDRICK TER BRUGGHEN, *Calling of Saint Matthew,* 1621. Oil on canvas, 3′ 4″ × 4′ 6″. Centraal Museum, Utrecht.

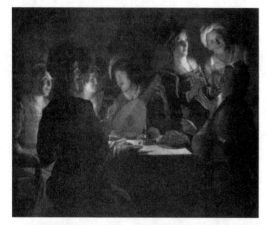

FIG. 25-08 GERRIT VAN HONTHORST, *Supper Party,* 1620. Oil on canvas, 4′ 8″ × 7″. Galleria degli Uffizi, Florence.

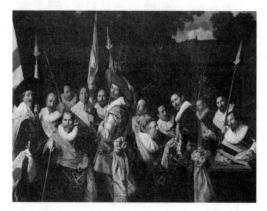

FIG. 25-09 FRANS HALS, *Archers of Saint Hadrian,* ca. 1633. Oil on canvas, 6′ 9″ × 11′. Frans Halsmuseum, Haarlem.

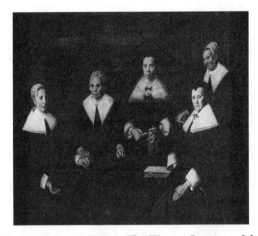

FIG. 25-10 FRANS HALS, *The Women Regents of the Old Men s Home at Haarlem,* 1664. Oil on canvas, 5′ 7″ × 8′ 2″. Frans Halsmuseum, Haarlem.

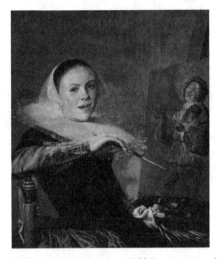

FIG. 25-11 JUDITH LEYSTER, *Self-Portrait,* ca. 1630. Oil on canvas, 2′ 5 3/8″ × 2′ 1 5/8″. National Gallery of Art, Washington, D.C. (gift of Mr. and Mrs. Robert Woods Bliss).

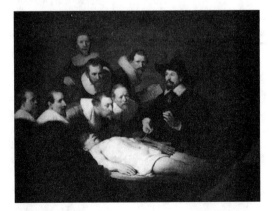

FIG. 25-12 REMBRANDT VAN RIJN, *Anatomy Lesson of Dr. Tulp,* 1632. Oil on canvas, 5′ 3 3/4″ × 7′ 1 1/4″. Mauritshuis, The Hague.

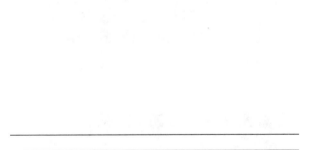

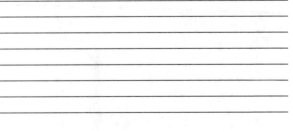

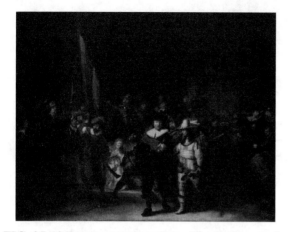

FIG. 25-13 REMBRANDT VAN RIJN, *The Company of Captain Frans Banning Cocq (Night Watch),* 1642. Oil on canvas, 11′ 11″ × 14′ 4″ (trimmed from original size). Rijksmuseum, Amsterdam.

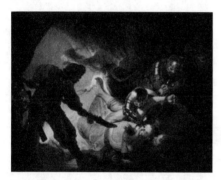

FIG. 25-13A REMBRANDT, Blinding of Samson, 1636.

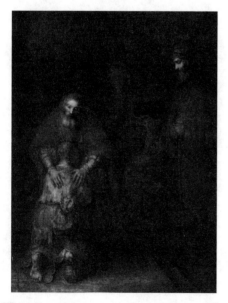

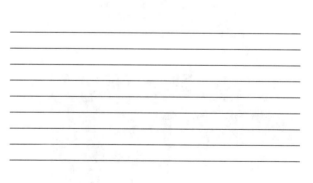

FIG. 25-14 REMBRANDT VAN RIJN, *Return of the Prodigal Son,* ca. 1665. Oil on canvas, 8′ 8″ × 6′ 9″. Hermitage Museum, Saint Petersburg.

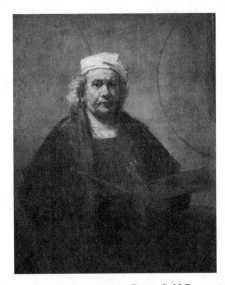

FIG. 25-15 Rembrandt van Rijn, *Self-Portrait,*
ca 1659–1660. Oil on canvas, 3′ 8 3/4″ × 3′ 1″.
Kenwood House, London (Iveagh Bequest).

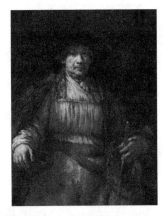

FIG. 25-15A Rembrandt, Self-Portrait, 1658.

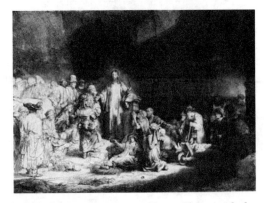

FIG. 25-16 Rembrandt van Rijn, *Christ with the
Sick around Him, Receiving the Children
(Hundred-Guilder Print),* ca. 1649. Etching.
11″ × 1′ 3 1/4″. Pierpont Morgan Library,
New York.

114

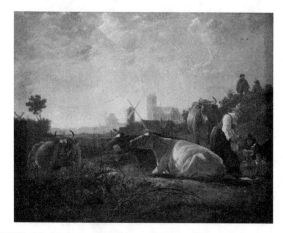

FIG. 25-17 AELBERT CUYP, *Distant View of Dordrecht, with a Milkmaid and Four Cows, and Other Figures,* (The "Large Dort") late 1640s. Oil on canvas, 5′ 1″ × 6′ 4 7/8″. National Gallery, London.

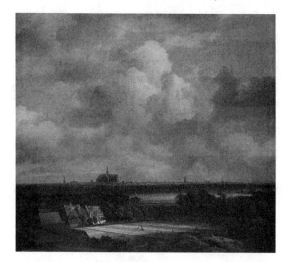

FIG. 25-18 JACOB VAN RUISDAEL, *View of Haarlem from the Dunes at Overveen,* ca. 1670. Oil on canvas, 1′ 10″ × 2″ 1″. Mauritshuis, The Hague.

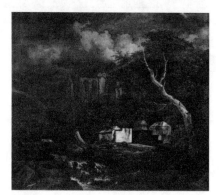

FIG. 25-18A RUSDAEL, Jewish Cemetery, ca 1655–1660.

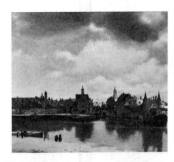

FIG. 25-18B VERMEER, View of Delft, ca. 1661.

_____
_____
_____
_____
_____
_____
_____
_____
_____
_____

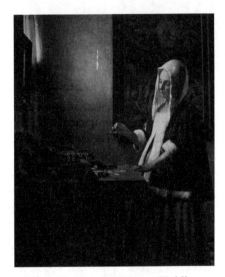

FIG. 25-19 JAN VERMEER, Woman Holding a
Balance, ca. 1664. Oil on canvas, 1′ 3 7/8″ × 1′ 2″.
National Gallery of Art, Washington, D.C.
(Widener Collection).

_____
_____
_____
_____
_____
_____
_____
_____
_____

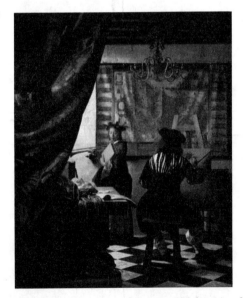

FIG. 25-20 JAN VERMEER, Allergory of the Art of
Paintings, 1670–1675. Oil on canvas, 4′4″ × 3′8′.
Kunsthistorisches Museum, Vienna.

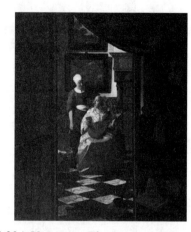

FIG. 25-20A VERMEER, The Letter, 1666.

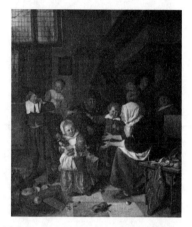

FIG. 25-21 JAN STEEN, Feast of Saint Nicholas, ca. 1660–1665. Oil on canvan, 2′8 1/4″ × 2′3 1/4″. Rijkamuseum, Amsterdam

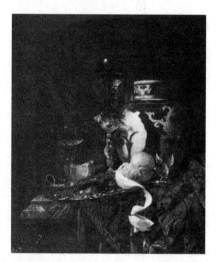

FIG. 25-22 WILLEM KALF, *Still Life with a Late Ming Ginger Jar,* 1669. Oil on canvas, 2′ 6″ × 2′ 1 3/4″. Indianapolis Museum of Art, Indianapolis (gift in commemoration of the 60th anniversary of the Art Association of Indianapolis, in memory of Daniel W. and Elizabeth C. Marmon).

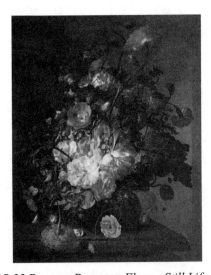

FIG. 25-23 RACHEL RUYSCH, *Flower Still Life,* after 1700. Oil on canvas, 2′ 5 3/4″ × 1″ 11 7/8″. Toledo Museum of Art, Toledo (purchased with funds from the Libbey Endowment, gift of Edward Drummond Libbey).

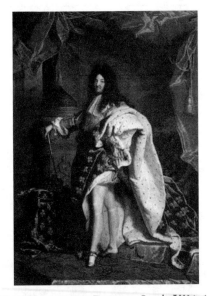

FIG. 25-24 HYACINTHE RIGUAD, Louis XIV, 1701. Oil on canvas, 9′2″ × 6′3″. Musee du Louvre, Paris.

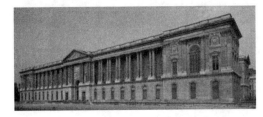

FIG. 25-25 CLAUDE PERRAULT, Louis Le Vau, and Charles Le Brun, east facade of the Louvre (looking southwest), Paris, France, 1667–1670.

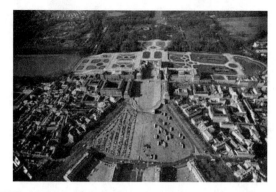

FIG. 25-26 Aerial view (looking west) of the palace and gardens, Versailles, France, begun 1669.

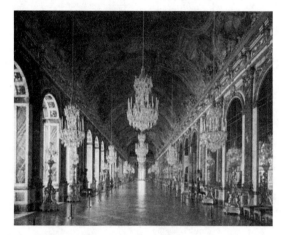

FIG. 25-27 JULES HARDOUIN-MANSART and CHARLES LE BRUN, Galerie des Glaces (Hall of Mirrors), palace of Louis XIV, Versailles, France, ca. 1680.

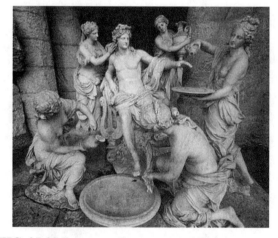

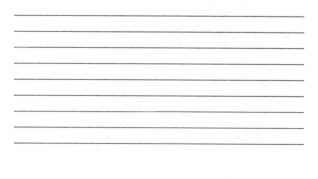

FIG. 25-28 FRANÇOIS GIRARDON and THOMAS REGNAUDIN, *Apollo Attended by the Nymphs,* Grotto of Thetis, Versailles, France, ca. 1666–1672. Marble, life-size.

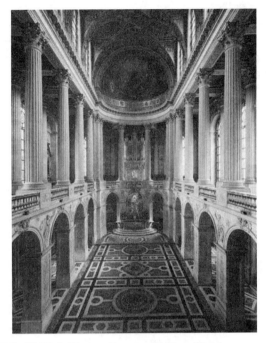

FIG. 25-29 J. ROYAL CHAPEL, with ceiling decorations by ANTOINE COYPEL, palace of Louis XIV, Versailles, France, 1698–1710.

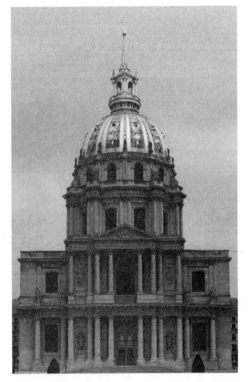

FIG. 25-30 JULES HARDOUIN-MANSART, Eglise du Dome (looking north), Church of the Invalides, Paris, France, 1676–1706.

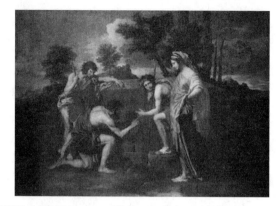

FIG. 25-31 NICOLAS POUSSIN, Etin Arcadia Ego, ca. 1665. Oil on canvas, 2′10″ × 4′. Musee du Louvre, Paris.

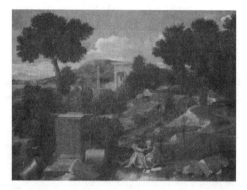

FIG. 25-32 NICOLAS POUSSIN, Landscape with Saint John on Patmos, 1640. Oil on canvas, 3′ 3 1/2″ × 4′ 5 5/8.″ Art Institute of Chicago, Chicago (A. A. Munger Collection)

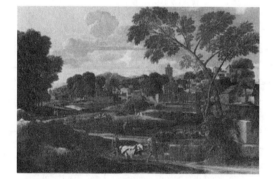

FIG. 25-32A POUSSIN, Burial of Phocion, 1648.

121

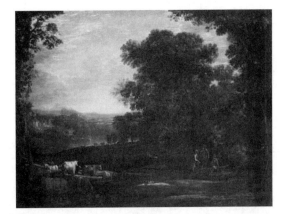

FIG. 25-33 CLAUDE LORRAIN, Landscape with Cattle
and Peasants, 1629. Oil on canvas, 3′6″ × 4′10 1/2″.
Philadelphia Museum of Art, Philadelphia
(George W. Elkins Collection).

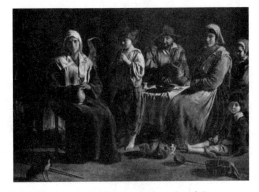

FIG. 25-34 LOUIS LE NATIN, *Family of Country
People*, ca 1640. Oil on canvas, 3′8″ × 5′2″.
Louvre, Paris.

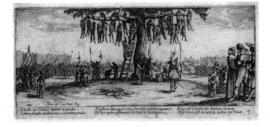

FIG. 25-35 JACQUES CALLOT, Hanging tree, from the
Miseries of War series, 1629–1633. Etiching.
3 3/4″ × 7 1/4″. Biliotheque Nationale, Paris.

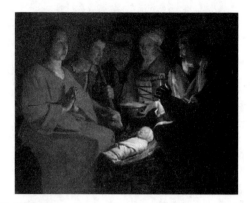

FIG. 25-36 GEORGES DE LA TOUR, *Adoration of the Shepherds,* 1645–1650. Oil on canvas, 3′ 6″ × 4′ 6″. Louvre, Paris.

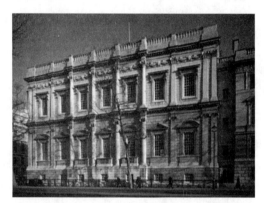

FIG. 25-37 INIGO JONES, Banqueting House (looking northeast).Whitehall, London, England 1619–1622.

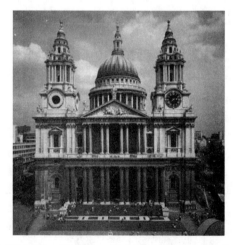

FIG. 25-38 SIR CHRISTOPHER WREN, west facade of Saint Paul's Cathedral, London, England 1675–1710.

Chapter 26

Rococo to Neoclassicism:
The 18th Century in Europe and America

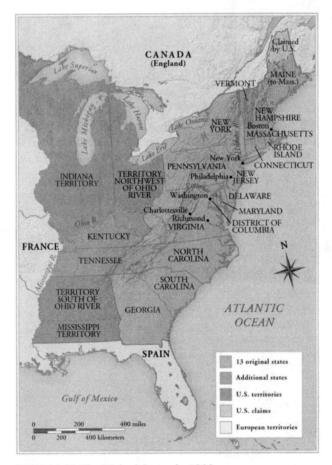

MAP 26-01 The United States in 1800.

_____

_____

_____

_____

_____

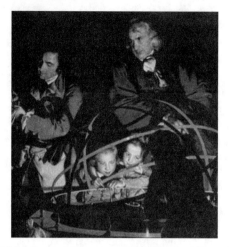

FIG. 26-01 JOSEPH WRIGHT of Derby, A philosopher Giving a Lecture at Orrerry, ca. 173-1765. Oil on canvas, 4/100 × 6980. Derby Museums and Art Gallery, Derby.

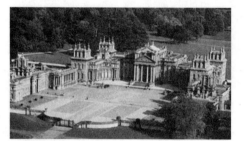

FIG. 26-01A VANBRUGH and HAWKSMOOR, Blenheim Palace, 1705–1725.

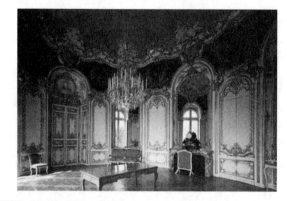

FIG. 26-02 GERMAIN BOFFRAND, Salon de la Princesse, with painting by CHARLES-JOSEPH NATOIRE and sculpture by J. B. LEMOINE, Hôtel de Soubise, Paris, France, 1737–1740.

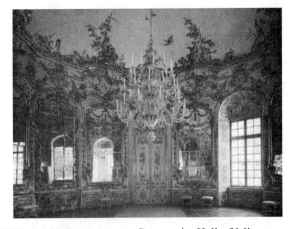

FIG. 26-03 FRANÇOIS DE CUVILLIÉS, Hall of Mirrors, the Amalienburg, Nymphenburg Palace park, Munich, Germany, early 18th century.

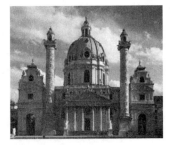

FIG. 26-03A FISCHER VON ERLACH, Karlskirche, Vienna, 1716–1737.

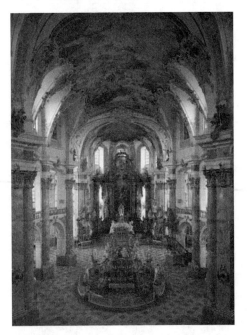

FIG. 26-04 BALTHASAR NEUMANN, interior of pilgrimage church of Vierzehnheiligen (looking east), near Staffelstein, Germany, 1743–1772.

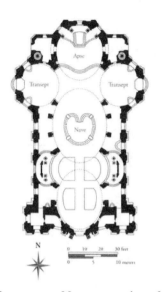

FIG. 26-05 BALTHASAR NEUMANN, plan of the pilgrimage church of Vierzehnheiligen, near Staffelstein, Germany, 1743–1772.

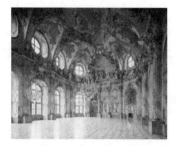

FIG. 26-05A NEUMANN, KAISERSAAL, WURZBURG, 1719–1744.

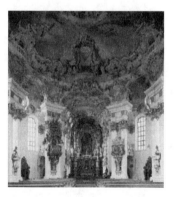

FIG. 26-05B ZIMMERMANN, WIESKIRCHE, FUSSEN, 1745–1754.

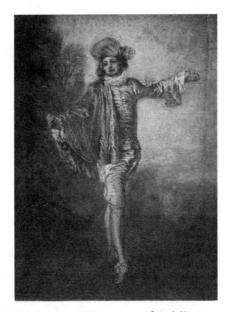

FIG. 26-06 ANTOINE WATTEAU, *L9Indifférent,* ca. 1716. Oil on canvas, 10″ × 7″. Musee du Louvre, Paris.

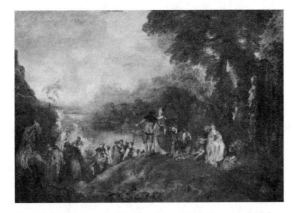

FIG. 26-07 ANTOINE WATTEAU, *Pilgrimage to Cythera,* 1717. Oil on canvas, 4′ 3″ × 6′ 4 1/2″. Musee du Louvre, Paris

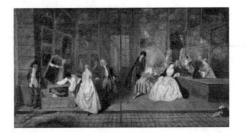

FIG. 26-07A WATTEAU, Signboard of Gersaint, 1721.

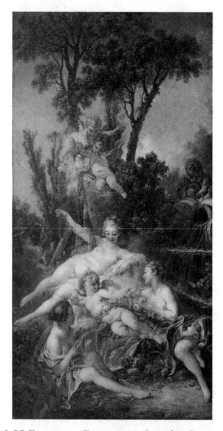

FIG. 26-08 FRANÇOIS BOUCHER, *Cupid a Captive,*
1754. Oil on canvas, 5′ 6″ × 2′ 10″. Wallace Collection,
London..

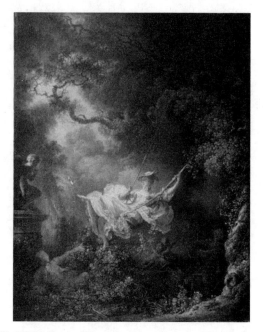

FIG. 26-09 JEAN- HONORE FRAGONARD, The Swing,
1766. Oil on canvas, 2′8 5/8″ × 2′2″. Wallace
Collection, London.

129

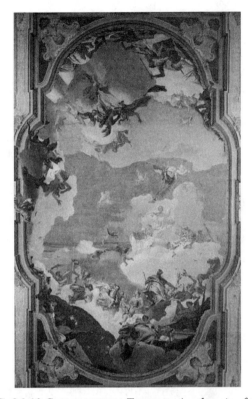

FIG. 26-10 GIAMBATTISTA TIEPOLO, *Apotheosis of the Pisani Family,* ceiling fresco in the Villa Pisani, Stra, Italy, 1761–1762. Fresco, 77′ 1″ × 44′ 3″.

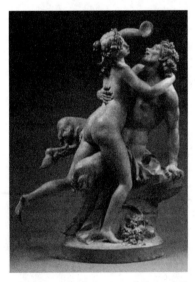

FIG. 26-11 CLOUDION, NYMPH and SATYR CAROUSING, ca. 1780–1790. Terracotta, 1′11 1/4″ high. Metropolitan Museum of Art, New York (bequest of Benjamin Altman, 1913).

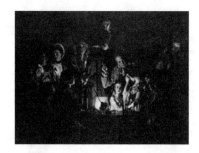

FIG. 26-11A WRIGHT OF DERBY, Experiment on a Bird, 1768.

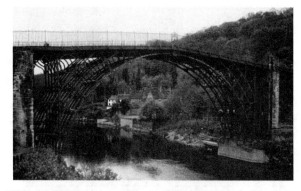

FIG. 26-12 ABRAHAM DARBY III and THOMAS F. PRITCHARD, iron bridge, (looking northwest) Coalbrookdale, England 1776–1779.

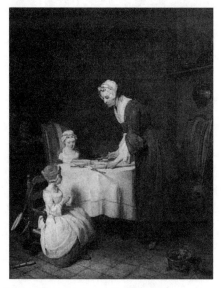

FIG. 26-13 JEAN-BAPTISTE-SIMÉON CHARDIN, *Saying Grace,* 1740. Oil on canvas, 1′ 7″ × 1′ 3″. Musee du Louvre, Paris.

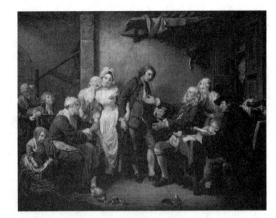

FIG. 26-14 JEAN-BAPTISTE GREUZE, *Village Bride,*
1761. Oil on canvas, 3′ × 3′ 10 1/2″.
Musee du Louvre, Paris.

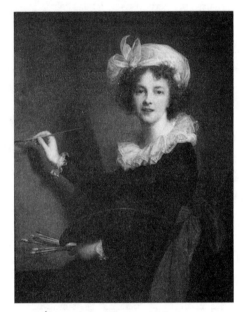

FIG. 26-15 ÉLISABETH LOUISE VIGÉE-LEBRUN,
Self-Portrait, 1790. Oil on canvas, 8′ 4″ × 6′ 9″.
Galleria degli Uffizi, Florence.

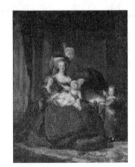

FIG. 26-15A VIGEE-LEBRUN, MARIE ANTOINETTE, 1787.

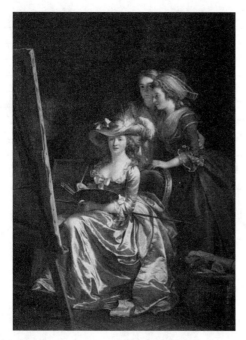

FIG. 26-16 ADÉLAÏDE LABILLE-GUIARD,
Self-Portrait with Two Pupils, 1785. Oil on canvas,
6′ 11″ × 4′ 11 1/2″. Metropolitan Museum of Art,
New York (gift of Julia A. Berwind 1953).

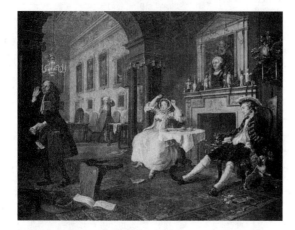

FIG. 26-17 WILLIAM HOGARTH, *Breakfast Scene,*
from *Marriage à la Mode,* ca. 1745. Oil on canvas,
2′ 4″ × 3′. National Gallery, London.

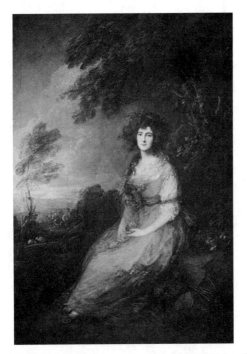

FIG. 26-18 THOMAS GAINSBOROUGH, *Mrs. Richard Brinsley Sheridan,* 1787. Oil on canvas, 7′ 2 5/8″ × 5′ 5/8″. National Gallery of Art, Washington, D.C. (Andrew W Mellon Collection).

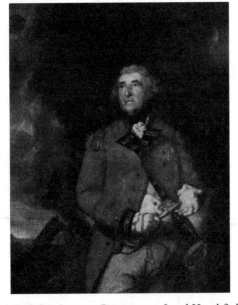

FIG. 26-19 SIR JOSHUA REYNOLDS, *Lord Heathfield,* 1787. Oil on canvas, 4′ 8″ × 3′ 9″. National Gallery, London.

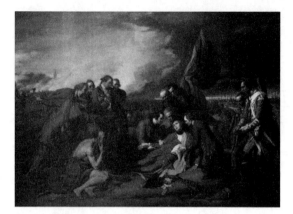

FIG. 26-20 BENJAMIN WEST, *Death of General Wolfe,*
1771. Oil on canvas, 4′ 11 1/2″ × 7′. National Gallery of
Canada, Ottawa (gift of the Duke of Westminster,
1918).

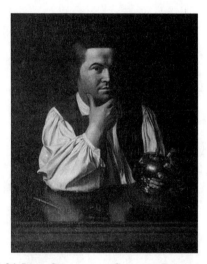

FIG. 26-21 JOHN SINGLETON COPLEY, *Portrait of Paul
Revere,* ca. 1768–1770. Oil on canvas, 2′ 11 1/8″ × 2′
4″. Museum of Fine Arts, Boston (gift of Joseph
W., William B., and Edward H. R. Revere).

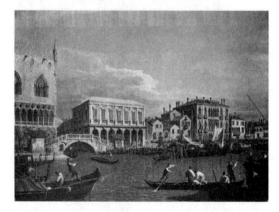

FIG. 26-22 ANTONIO CANALETTO, *Riva degli
Schiavoni, Venice,* ca. 1735–1740. Oil on canvas,
1′ 6 1/2″ × 2′ 7/8″. Toledo Museum of Art, Toledo.

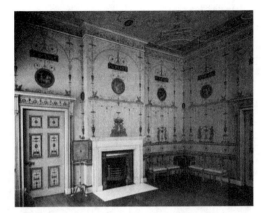

FIG. 26-23 ROBERT ADAM, Etruscan Room, from Osterley Park House, Middlesex, England begun 1761. Reconstructed in the Victoria & Albert Museum, London.

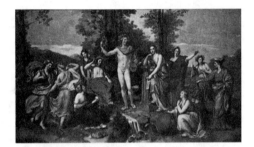

FIG. 26-23A Mengs, Parnassus, 1761.

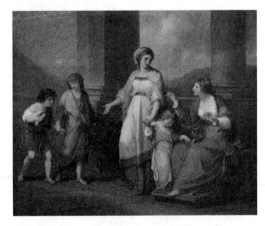

FIG. 26-24 ANGELICA KAUFFMANN, *Cornelia Presenting Her Children as Her Treasures,* or *Mother of the Gracchi,* ca. 1785. Oil on canvas, 3′ 4″ × 4′ 2″. Virginia Museum of Fine Arts, Richmond (the Adolph D. and Wilkins C. Williams Fund).

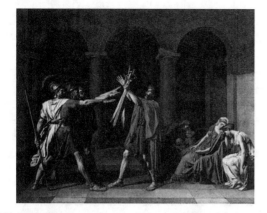

FIG. 26-25 JACQUES-LOUIS DAVID, *Oath of the Horatii,*
1784. Oil on canvas, 10′ 10″ × 13′ 11″.
Musee du Louvre, Paris.

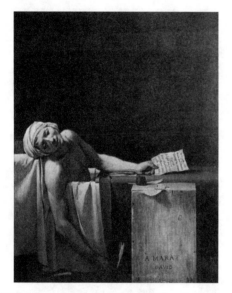

FIG. 26-26 JACQUES-LOUIS DAVID, *Death of Marat,*
1793. Oil on canvas, 5′ 5″ × 4′ 2 1/2″. Musée Royaux
des Beaux-Arts de Belgique, Brussels.

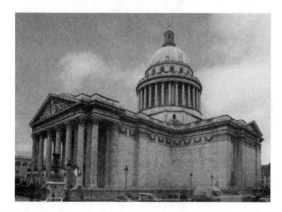

FIG. 26-27 JACQUES-GERMAIN SOUFFLOT, Pantheon
(Sainte-Genevieve; looking northeast), Paris, France,
1755–1792.

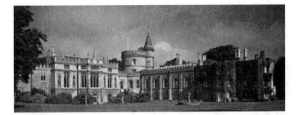

FIG. 26-27A Walpole, Strawberry Hill, Twickenham, 1749–1777.

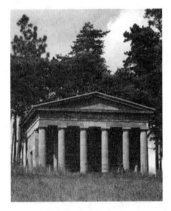

FIG. 26-28 RICHARD BOYLE and WILLIAM KENT, Chiswick House (looking northwest), near London, England, begun 1725.

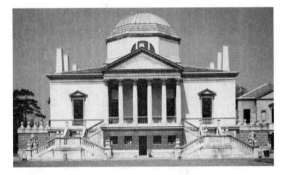

FIG. 26-28A STUART, Doric Protico Hagley Park, 1758.

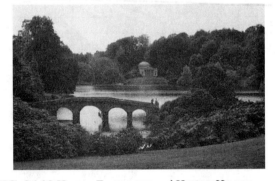

FIG. 26-29 HENRY FLITCROFT and HENRY HOARE, the park at Stourhead England 1743–1765.

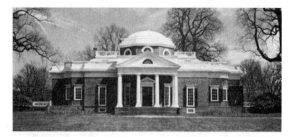

FIG. 26-30 THOMAS JEFFERSON, Monticello, Charlottesville, Virginia, 1770–1806.

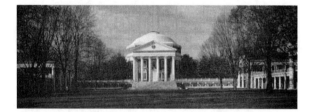

FIG. 26-31 THOMAS JEFFERSON, Rotunda and Lawn, (looking north) University of Virginia, Charlottesville, Virginia, 1819–1826.

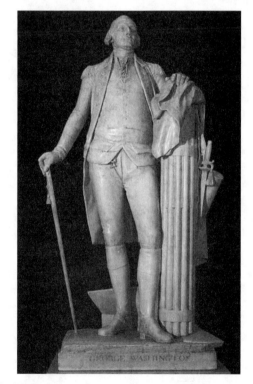

FIG. 26-32 JEAN-ANTOINE HOUDON, *George Washington,* 1788–1792. Marble, 6′ 2″ high. State Capitol, Richmond.

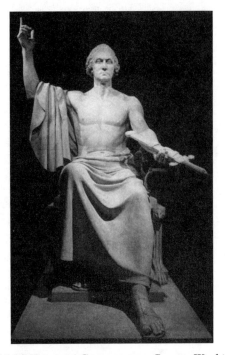

FIG. 26-33 HORATIO GREENOUGH, *George Washington,*
1840. Marble, 11′ 4″ high. Smithsonian American
Art Museum, Washington, D.C.

Chapter 27

Romanticism, Realism, Photography: Europe and America 1800 to 1870

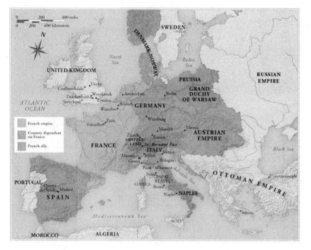

Map 27-01 The Napoleonic Empire in 1815.

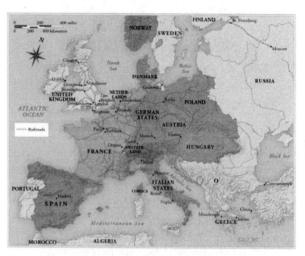

Map 27-02 Europe around 1850.

_____

_____

_____

_____

_____

_____

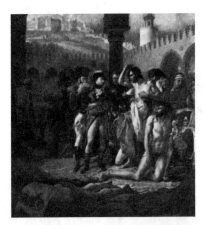

FIG. 27-01 ANTOINE-JEAN GROS, NAPOLEON at the Plague House at Jaffa, 1804. Oil on canvas, 17′5″ × 23′7″. Musee du Louvre, Paris.

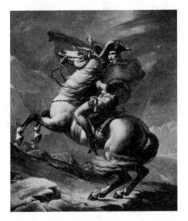

FIG. 27-01A DAVID, Napoleon Crossing Saint-Bernard, 1800-1801.

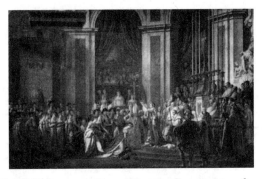

FIG. 27-02 JACQUES-LOUIS DAVID, *Coronation of Napoleon,* 1805–1808. Oil on canvas, 20′ 4 1/2″ × 32′ 1 3/4″. Musee du Louvre, Paris.

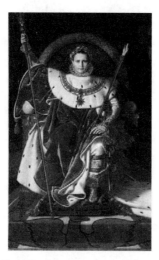

FIG. 27-02A INGRES, NAPOLEON on His Imperial Throne, 1806.

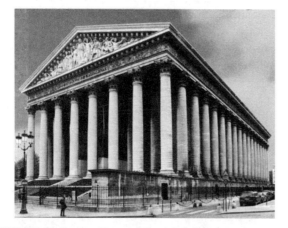

FIG. 27-03 PIERRE VIGNON, La Madeleine, Paris, France, 1807–1842.

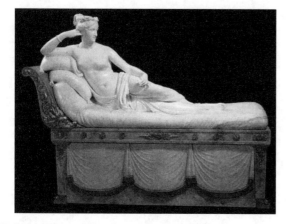

FIG. 27-04 ANTONIO CANOVA, *Pauline Borghese as Venus,* 1808. Marble, 6′ 7″ long. Galleria Borghese, Rome.

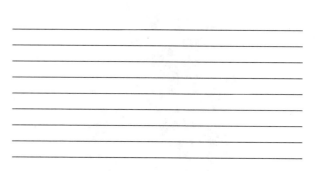

143

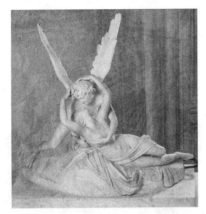

FIG. 27-04A CANOVA, Cupid and Psyche, 1787–1793.

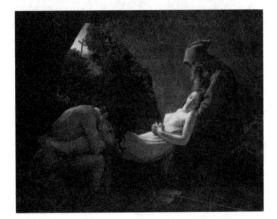

FIG. 27-05 ANNE-LOUIS GIRODET-TRIOSON, *Burial of Atala,* 1808. Oil on canvas, 6′ 11″ × 8′ 9″. Musee du Louvre, Paris.

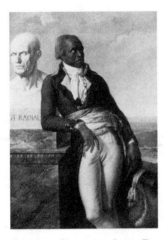

FIG. 27-05A GIRODET-TRIOSON, JEAN-BAPTISTE BELLEY, 1797.

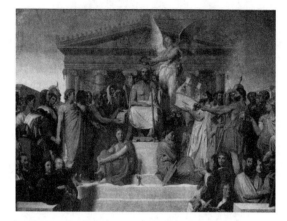

FIG. 27-06 JEAN-AUGUSTE-DOMINIQUE INGRES, *Apotheosis of Homer,* 1827. Oil on canvas, 12′ 8″ × 16′ 10 3/4″. Musee du Louvre, Paris.

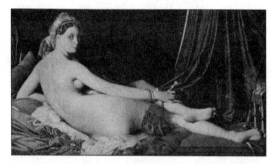

FIG. 27-07 JEAN-AUGUSTE-DOMINIQUE INGRES, *Grande Odalisque,* 1814. Oil on canvas, 2′ 11 7/8″ × 5′ 4″. Musee du Louvre, Paris.

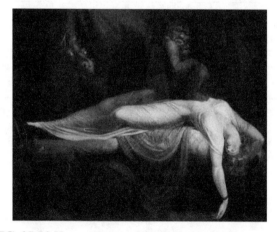

FIG. 27-08 HENRY FUSELI, *The Nightmare,* 1781. Oil on canvas, 3′ 3 3/4″ × 4′ 1 1/2″. Detroit Institute of the Arts (Founders Society Purchase with funds from Mr. and Mrs. Bert L. Smokler and Mr. and Mrs. Lawrence A. Fleishman).

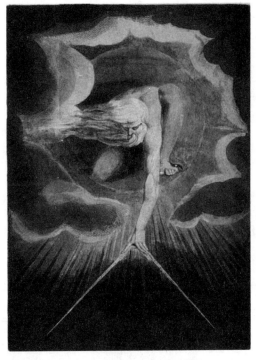

FIG. 27-09 WILLIAM BLAKE, *Ancient of Days,*
frontispiece *of Europe: A Prophecy,* 1794. Metal relief
etching, hand colored 9 1/2″ × 6 3/4″. Pierpont Morgan
Library, New York.

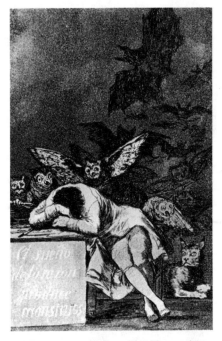

FIG. 27-10 FRANCISCO GOYA, *The Sleep of Reason
Produces Monsters,* from *Los Caprichos,* ca. 1798.
Etching and aquatint, 8 1/2″ × 5 7/8″. Metropolitan
Museum of Art, New York (gift of M. Knoedler & Co.,
1918).

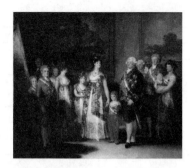

FIG. 27-10A GOYA, Family of Charles IV, 1800.

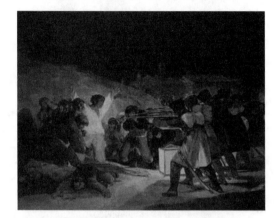

FIG. 27-11 FRANCISCO GOYA, *Third of May, 1808,* 1814–1815. Oil on canvas, 8′ 9″ × 13′ 4″. Museo del Prado, Madrid.

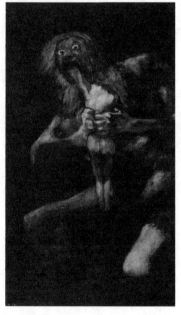

FIG. 27-12 FRANCISCO GOYA, *Saturn Devouring One of His Children,* 1819–1823. Detached fresco mounted on canvas, 4′ 9 1/8″ × 2′ 8 5/8″. Museo del Prado, Madrid.

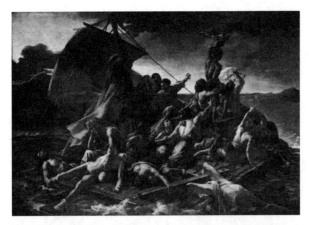

FIG. 27-13 THÉODORE GÉRICAULT, *Raft of the Medusa,* 1818–1819. Oil on canvas, 16′ 1″ × 23′ 6″. Musee du Louvre, Paris.

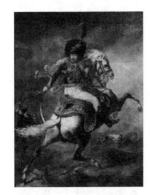

FIG. 27-13A GERICAULT, Charging Chasseut, 1812.

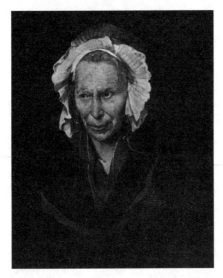

FIG. 27-14 THÉODORE GÉRICAULT, *Insane Woman,* 1822–1823. Oil on canvas, 2′ 4″ × 1′ 9″. Musée des Beaux-Arts, Lyons.

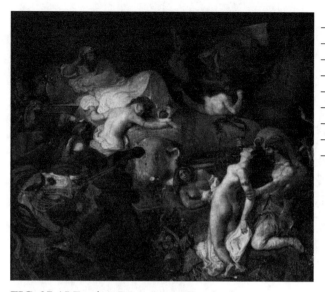

FIG. 27-15 EUGÈNE DELACROIX, *Death of Sardanapalus,* 1827. Oil on canvas, 12′ 1 1/2″ × 16′ 2 7/8″. Musee du Louvre, Paris.

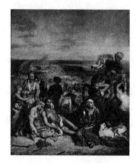

FIG. 27-15A DELACROUX, Massacre at Chios, 1822–1824.

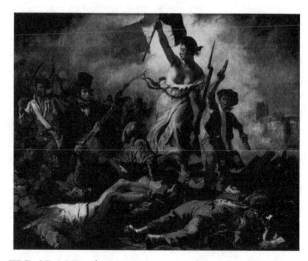

FIG. 27-16 EUGÈNE DELACROIX, *Liberty Leading the People,* 1830. Oil on canvas, 8′ 6″ × 10′ 8″. Musee du Louvre, Paris.

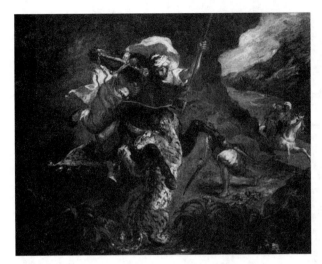

FIG. 27-17 EUGÈNE DELACROIX, *Tiger Hunt,* 1854. Oil on canvas, 2′ 5″ × 3′. Musée d'Orsay, Paris.

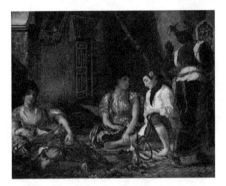

FIG. 27-17A DELACROUIX, Women of Algeria, 1834.

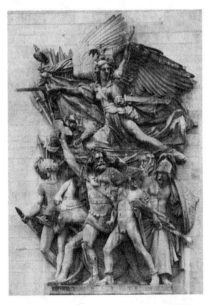

FIG. 27-18 FRANÇOIS RUDE, *Departure of the Volunteers of 1792 (La Marseillaise),* Arc de Triomphe, Paris, France, 1833-1836. Limestone, 41′ 8″ high.

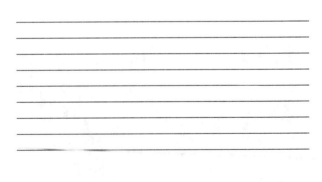

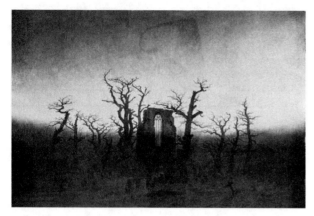

FIG. 27-19 CASPAR DAVID FRIEDRICH, *Abbey in the Oak Forest,* 1810. Oil on canvas, 3′ 7 1/2″ × 5′ 7 1/4″. Nationalgalerie, Staatliche Museen zu Berlin, Berlin.

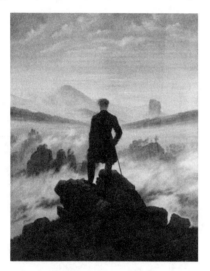

FIG. 27-20 CASPAR DAVID FRIEDRICH, Wanderer above a Sea of Mist, 1817–1818. Oil on canvas, 3′ 1 3/4″ × 2′ 5 3/8″. Hamburger Kunsthalle, Hamburg.

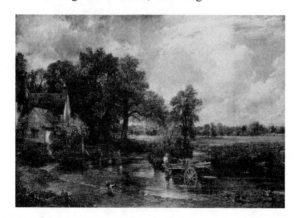

FIG. 27-21 JOHN CONSTABLE, *The Haywain,* 1821. Oil on canvas, 4′ 3″ × 6′ 2″. National Gallery, London.

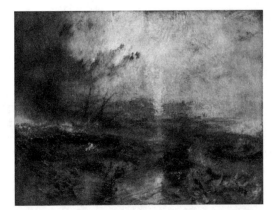

FIG. 27-22 JOSEPH MALLORD WILLIAM TURNER, *The Slave Ship (Slavers Throwing Overboard the Dead and Dying, Typhoon Coming On)*, 1840. Oil on canvas, 2′ 11 11/16″ × 4′ 5/16″. Museum of Fine Arts, Boston (Henry Lillie Pierce Fund).

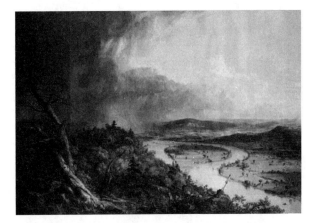

FIG. 27-23 THOMAS COLE, *The Oxbow (View from Mount Holyoke, Northampton, Massachusetts, after a Thunderstorm)*, 1836. Oil on canvas, 4′ 3 1/2″ × 6′ 4″. Metropolitan Museum of Art, New York (gift of Mrs. Russell Sage, 1908).

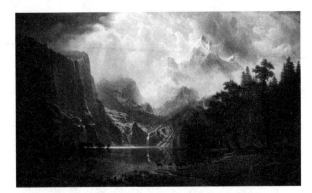

FIG. 27-24 ALBERT BIERSTADT, *Among the Sierra Nevada Mountains, California,* 1868. Oil on canvas, 6′ × 10′. National Museum of American Art, Smithsonian Institution, Washington, D.C.

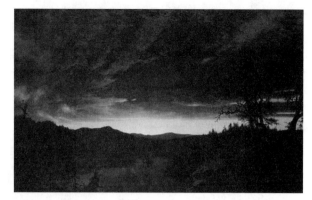

FIG. 27-25 FREDERIC EDWIN CHURCH, *Twilight in the Wilderness,* 1860s. Oil on canvas, 3′ 4″ × 5′ 4″. Cleveland Museum of Art, Cleveland (Mr. and Mrs. William H. Marlatt Fund 1965.233).

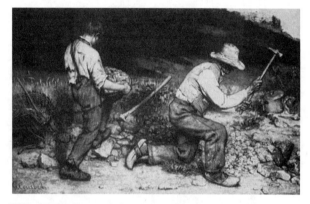

FIG. 27-26 GUSTAV COURBET, *The Stone Breakers,* 1849. Oil on canvas, 5′ 3″ × 8′ 6″. Formerly Gemäldegalerie, Dresden (destroyed in 1945).

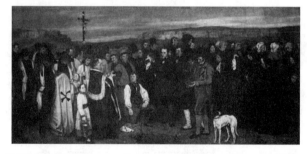

FIG. 27-27 GUSTAVE COURBET, *Burial at Ornans,* 1849. Oil on canvas, 10′ 3 1/2″ × 21′ 9 1/2″. Musée d'Orsay, Paris.

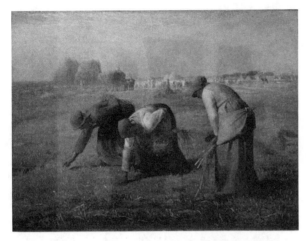

FIG. 27-28 JEAN-FRANÇOIS MILLET, *The Gleaners,* 1857. Oil on canvas, 2′ 9″ × 3′ 8″. Musée d'Orsay, Paris.

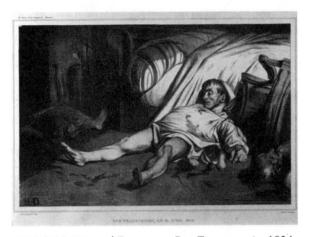

FIG. 27-29 HONORÉ DAUMIER, *Rue Transnonain,* 1834. Lithograph, 1′ × 1′ 5 1/2″. Philadelphia Museum of Art, Philadelphia (bequest of Fiske and Marie Kimball).

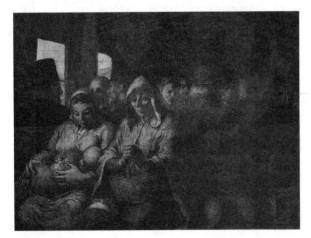

FIG. 27-30 HONORÉ DAUMIER, *Third-Class Carriage,* ca. 1862. Oil on canvas, 2′ 1 3/4″ × 2′ 11 1/2″. Metropolitan Museum of Art, New York (H. O. Havemeyer Collection, bequest of Mrs. H. O. Havemeyer, 1929).

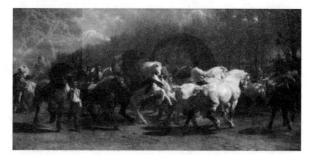

FIG. 27-31 ROSA BONHEUR, *The Horse Fair,*
1853–1855. Oil on canvas, 8′ 1/4″ × 16′ 7 1/2″.
Metropolitan Museum of Art, New York (gift of
Cornelius Vanderbilt, 1887).

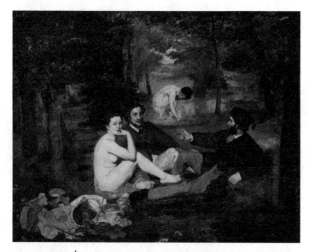

FIG. 27-32 ÉDOUARD MANET, *Le Déjeuner sur l'Herbe
(Luncheon on the Grass),* 1863. Oil on canvas,
7′ × 8′ 8″. Musée d'Orsay, Paris.

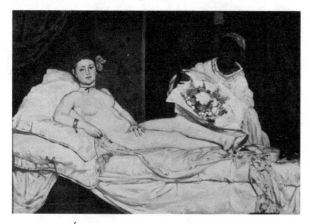

FIG. 27-33 ÉDOUARD MANET, *Olympia,* 1863.
Oil on canvas, 4′ 3″ × 6′ 2 1/4″. Musée d'Orsay, Paris.

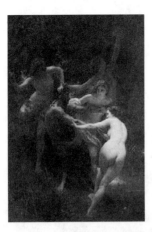

FIG. 27-33A BOUGUEREAU, Nymphs and a Satyr, 1873.

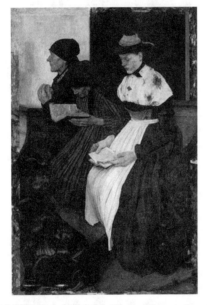

FIG. 27-34 WILHELM LEIBL, *Three Women in a Village Church,* 1878–1882. Oil on canvas, 2′ 5″ × 2′ 1″. Kunsthalle, Hamburg.

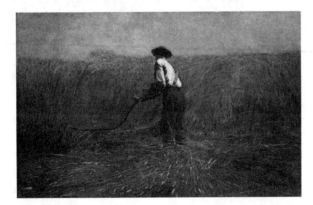

FIG. 27-35 WINSLOW HOMER, *Veteran in a New Field,* 1865. Oil on canvas, 2′ 1/8″ × 3′ 2 1/8″. Metropolitan Museum of Art, New York (bequest of Miss Adelaide Milton de Groot, 1967).

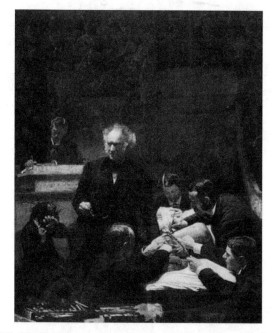

FIG. 27-36 THOMAS EAKINS, *The Gross Clinic,* 1875. Oil on canvas, 8′ × 6′ 6″. Philadelphia Museum of Art, Philadelphia.

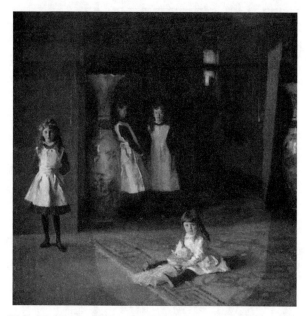

FIG. 27-37 JOHN SINGER SARGENT, *The Daughters of Edward Darley Boit,* 1882. Oil on canvas, 7′ 3 3/8″ × 7′ 3 5/8″. Museum of Fine Arts, Boston (gift of Mary Louisa Boit, Florence D. Boit, Jane Hubbard Boit, and Julia Overing Boit, in memory of their father, Edward Darley Boit).

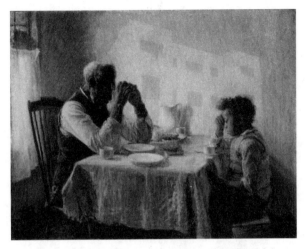

FIG. 27-38 Henry Ossawa Tanner, *The Thankful Poor,* 1894. Oil on canvas, 2′ 11 1/2″ × 3′ 8 1/4″. Collection of William H. and Camille Cosby.

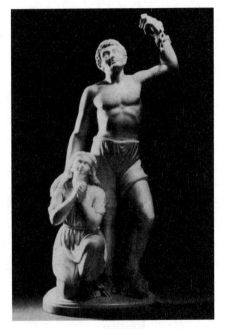

FIG. 27-39 Edmonia Lewis, *Forever Free,* 1867. Marble, 3′ 5 1/4″ high. James A. Porter Gallery of Afro-American Art, Howard University, Washington, D.C.

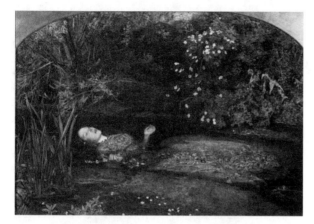

FIG. 27-40 JOHN EVERETT MILLAIS, *Ophelia,* 1852. Oil on canvas, 2′ 6″ × 3′ 8″. Tate Gallery, London.

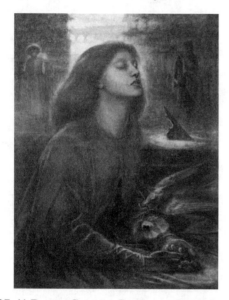

FIG. 27-41 DANTE GABRIEL ROSSETTI, *Beata Beatrix,* ca. 1863. Oil on canvas, 2′ 10″ × 2′ 2″. Tate Gallery, London.

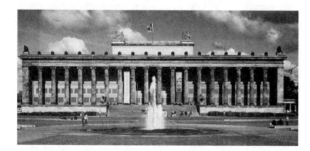

FIG. 27-42 KARL FRIEDRICH SCHINKEL, Altes Museum, Berlin, Germany, 1822–1830.

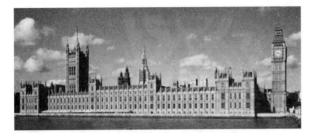

FIG. 27-43 CHARLES BARRY and A.W.N. PUGIN,
Houses of Parliament, London, England designed 1835.

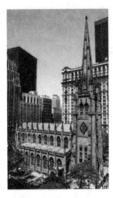

FIG. 27-43A RICHARD UPJOHN, Trinity Church, New
York, New York, 1841–1852.

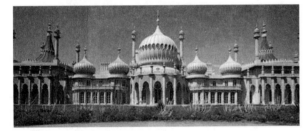

FIG. 27-44 JOHN NASH, Royal Pavilion, Brighton,
England, 1815–1818.

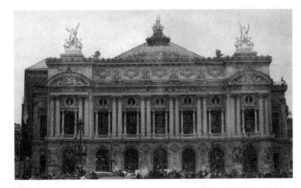

FIG. 27-45 CHARLES GERNIER, Opera (looking north),
Paris, France, 1861–1874.

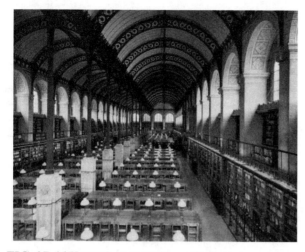

FIG. 27-46 HENRI LABROUSTE, reading room of the Bibliothèque Sainte-Geneviève, Paris, France, 1843–1850.

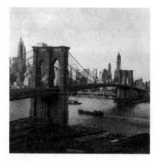

FIG. 27-46A ROEBLING, Brooklyn Bridge, 1867–1883.

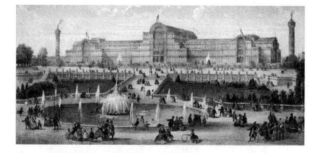

FIG. 27-47 JOSEPH PAXTON, Crystal Palace, London, England 1850–1851; enlarged and relocated at Sydenham, England 1852–1854. Detail of a color lithograph by ACHILLE-LOUIS MARTINET, ca. 1862. Private collection.

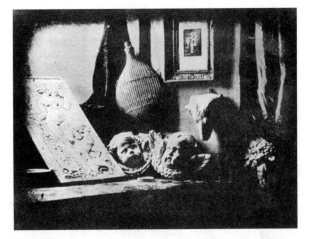

FIG. 27-48 Louis-Jacques-Mandé Daguerre, *Still Life in Studio,* 1837. Daguerreotype, 6 1/4″ × 8 1/4″. Société Française de Photographie, Paris.

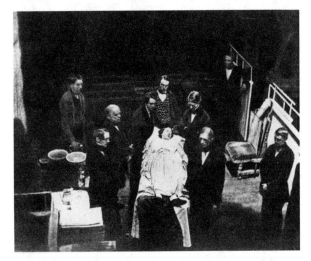

FIG. 27-49 Josiah Johnson Hawes and Albert Sands Southworth, *Early Operation under Ether, Massachusetts General Hospital,* ca. 1847. Daguerreotype, 6 1/2″ × 8 1/2″. Massachusetts General Hospital Archives and Special Collections, Boston.

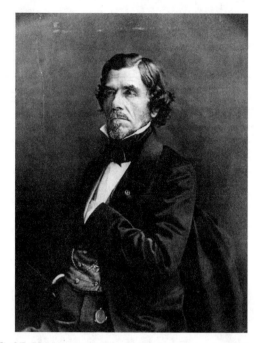

FIG. 27-50 NADAR, EUGENE DELACROIX, ca. 1855.
Modern print, 8 1/2″′ × 2/3″, from the original negative.
Bibliotheque Nationale, Paris.

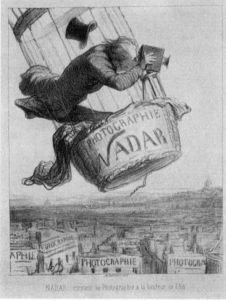

FIG. 27-51 HONORE DAUMIER, Nadar Raising
Photography to the Height of Art, 1862. Lithograph,
10 3/4″ × 8 3/4″. Museum of Fine Arts, Boston.

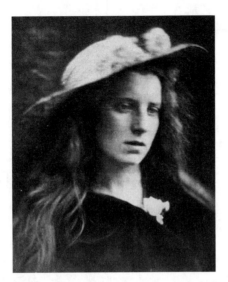

FIG. 27-52 JULIA MARGARET CAMERON, *Ophelia, Study No. 2,* 1867. Albumen print, 1′ 1 ″ × 10 2/3″. George Eastman House, Rochester (gift of Eastman Kodak Company; formerly Gabriel Cromer Collection).

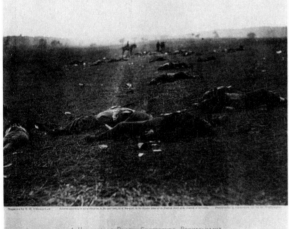

FIG. 27-53 TIMOTHY O′SULLIVAN, *A Harvest of Death, Gettysburg, Pennsylvania, July 1863,* 1863. Negative by Timothy O'Sullivan. Albumen print by ALEXANDER GARDNER, 6 3/4″ × 8 3/4″. New York Public Library (Astor, Lenox and Tilden Foundations, Rare Books and Manuscript Division), New York.

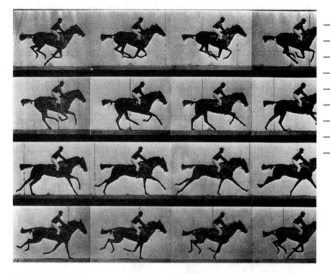

FIG. 27-54 EADWEARD MUYBRIDGE, *Horse Galloping,*
1878. Calotype print, 9″ × 12″. George Eastman House,
Rochester.

Chapter 28

Impressionism, Post-Impressionism, Symbolism: Europe and America, 1870 to 1900

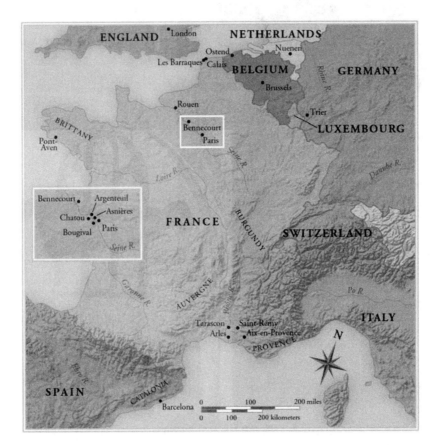

MAP 28-01 France around 1870.

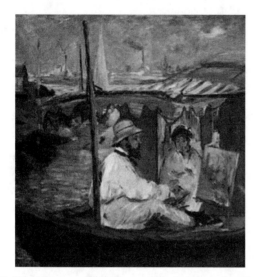

FIG. 28-01 EDOUARD MANET, Claude Monet in His Studio Boat, 1874. Oil on canvas, 2′8″ × 3′3 1/4″. Neue Pinakothek, Munich.

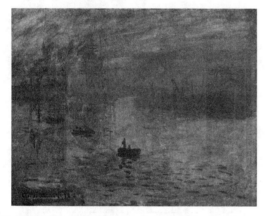

FIG. 28-02 CLAUDE MONET, *Impression: Sunrise,* 1872, Oil on canvas, 1′ 7 1/2″ × 2′ 1 1/2″. Musée Marmottan, Paris.

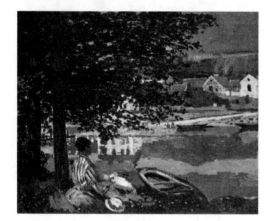

FIG. 28-02A MONET, Bank of the Seine, Bennecourt, 1868.

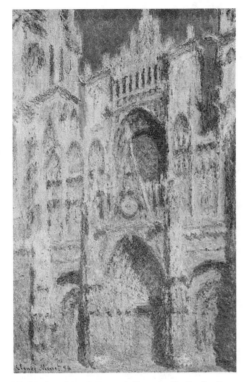

FIG. 28-03 CLAUDE MONET, *Rouen Cathedral:*
The Portal (in Sun), 1894. Oil on canvas,
3′ 3 1/4″ × 2′ 1 7/8″. Metropolitan Museum of Art,
New York (Theodore M. Davis Collection, bequest of
Theodore M. Davis, 1915).

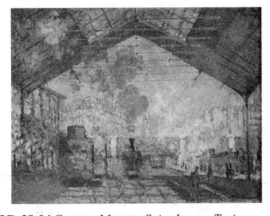

FIG. 28-04 CLAUDE MONET, *Saint-Lazare Train*
Station, 1877. Oil on canvas, 2′ 5 3/4″ × 3′ 5″.
Musée d'Orsay, Paris.

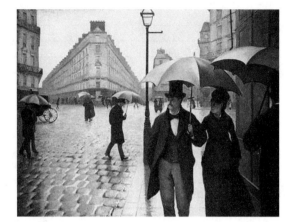

FIG. 28-05 GUSTAVE CAILLEBOTTE, *Paris: A Rainy Day,* 1877. Oil on canvas, 6′ 9″ × 9′ 9″. Art Institute of Chicago, Chicago (Worcester Fund).

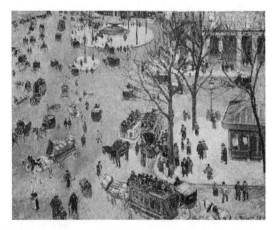

FIG. 28-06 CAMILLE PISSARRO, *La Place du Théâtre Français,* 1898. Oil on canvas, 2′ 4 1/2″ × 3′ 1/2″. Los Angeles County Museum of Art, Los Angeles (Mr. and Mrs. George Gard De Sylva Collection).

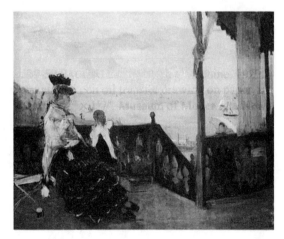

FIG. 28-07 BERTHE MORISOT, *Villa at the Seaside,* 1874. Oil on canvas, 1′ 7 3/4″ × 2′ 1/8″. Norton Simon Art Foundation, Los Angeles.

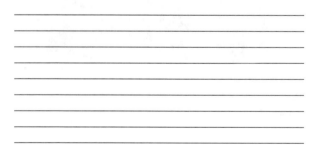

169

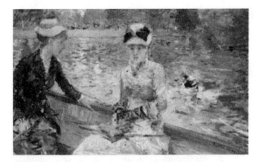

FIG. 28-07A MORISOR, Summer's Day. 1879.

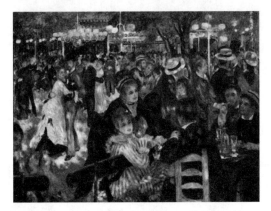

FIG. 28-08 PIERRE-AUGUSTE RENOIR, *Le Moulin de la Galette,* 1876. Oil on canvas, 4′ 3″ × 5′ 8″. Musée d'Orsay, Paris.

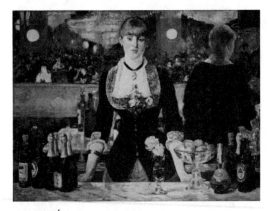

FIG. 28-09 ÉDOUARD MANET, *Bar at the Folies-Bergère,* 1882. Oil on canvas, 3′ 1″ × 4′ 3″. Courtauld Insitute of Art Gallery, London.

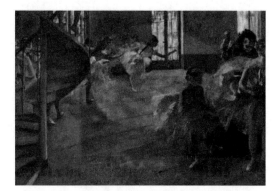

FIG. 28-10 EDGAR DEGAS, The Rehearsal 1874.
Oil on canvas, 1′ 11″ × 2′ 9″. Glasgow Art Galleries
and Museum, Glasgow (Burrell Collection).

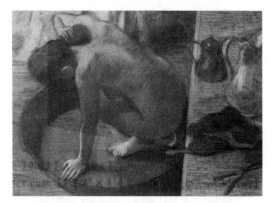

FIG. 28-11 EDGAR DEGAS, The Tub, 1886,
1′ 11 1/2″ × 2′ 8 3/8″. Musee d'Orsay, Paris.

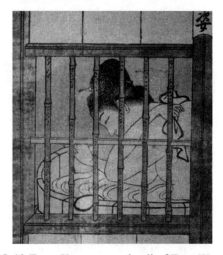

FIG. 28-12 TORII KIYONAGA, detail of Two Women at
the Bath, ca. 1780. Color woodblock, full print
10 1/2″ × 7 1/2, ″ detail 3 3/4″ × 3 1/2. ″ Musee
Guimet, Paris.

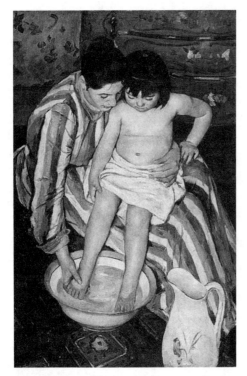

FIG. 28-13 MARY CASSATT, *The Bath,* ca. 1892.
Oil on canvas, 3′ 3″ × 2′ 2″. Art Institute of Chicago,
Chicago (Robert A. Walker Fund).

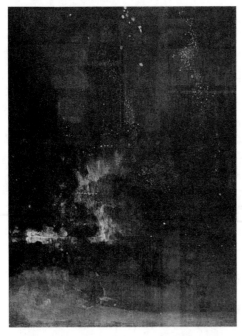

FIG. 28-14 JAMES ABBOTT MCNEILL WHISTLER,
Nocturne in Black and Gold (The Falling Rocket),
ca. 1875. Oil on panel, 1′11 5/8″ × 1′ 6 1/2″. Detroit
Institute of Arts, Detroit (gift of Dexter M. Ferry Jr.).

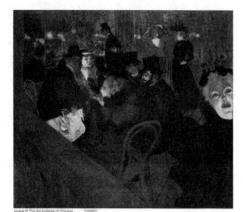

FIG. 28-15 HENRI DE TOULOUSE-LAUTREC, *At the Moulin Rouge,* 1892–1895. Oil on canvas, 4′ × 4′ 7″. Art Institute of Chicago, Chicago (Helen Birch Bartlett Memorial Collection).

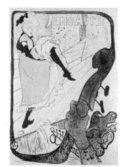

FIG. 28-15A TOULOUSE-LAUTREC, Jane Avril, 1893.

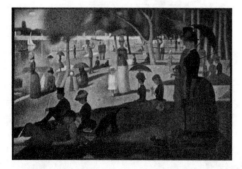

FIG. 28-16 GEORGES SEURAT, *A Sunday on La Grande Jatte,* 1884–1886. Oil on canvas, 6′ 9″ × 10′. Art Institute of Chicago, Chicago (Helen Birch Bartlett Memorial Collection, 1926.

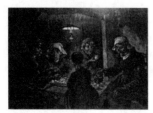

FIG. 28-16A VAN GOGH, The Potato Eaters, 1885.

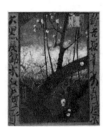

FIG. 28-16B VAN GOGH, Flowering Plum Tree, 1887.

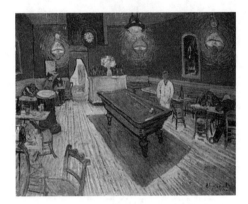

FIG. 28-17 VINCENT VAN GOGH, *Night Café,* 1888.
Oil on canvas, 2′ 4 1/2″ × 3′. Yale University
Art Gallery, New Haven (bequest of Stephen
Carlton Clark).

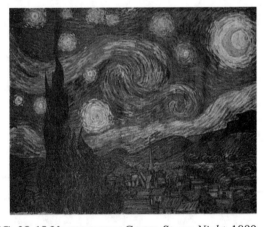

FIG. 28-18 VINCENT VAN GOGH, *Starry Night,* 1889.
Oil on canvas, 2′ 5″ × 3′ 1/4″. Museum of Modern
Art, New York (acquired through the Lillie P. Bliss
Bequest).

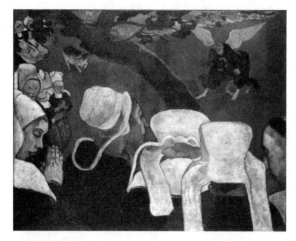

FIG. 28-19 PAUL GAUGUIN, *Vision after the Sermon, or Jacob Wrestling with the Angel,* 1888. Oil on canvas, 2′ 4 3/4″ × 3′ 1/2″. National Gallery of Scotland Edinburgh.

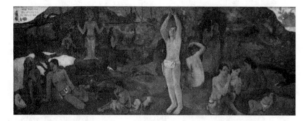

FIG. 28-20 PAUL GAUGUIN, *Where Do We Come From? What Are We? Where Are We Going?* 1897. Oil on canvas, 4′ 6 3/4″ × 12′ 3″. Museum of Fine Arts, Boston (Tompkins Collection).

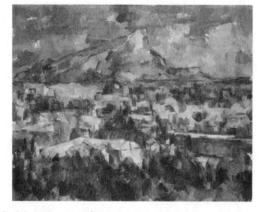

FIG. 28-21 PAUL CÉZANNE, *Mount Sainte-Victoire,* 1902–1904. Oil on canvas, 2′ 3 1/2″ × 2′ 11 1/4″. Philadelphia Museum of Art, Philadelphia (The George W. Elkins Collection).

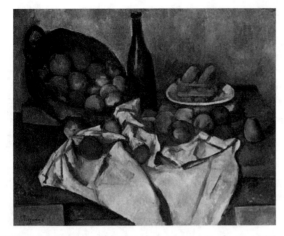

FIG. 28-22 PAUL CÉZANNE, *The Large Bathers,* 1906. Oil on canvas, 6′ 10 7/8″ × 8′ 2 3/4″. Philadelphia Museum of Art, Philadelphia (W.P Wilstach Collection).

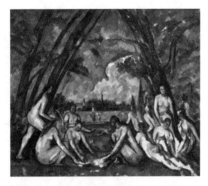

FIG. 28-22A CEZANNE, Large Bathers, 1906.

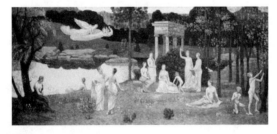

FIG. 28-23 PIERRE PUVIS DE CHAVANNES, *Sacred Grove,* 1884. Oil on canvas, 2′ 11 1/2″ × 6′ 10″. Art Institute of Chicago, Chicago (Potter Palmer Collection).

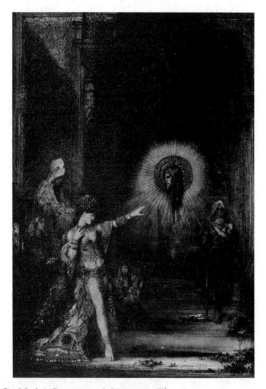

FIG. 28-24 GUSTAVE MOREAU, *The Apparition.*
1874–1876. Watercolor on paper, 3′ 5 3/4″ × 2′ 4 3/8″.
Musee du Louvre, Paris.

_____
_____
_____
_____
_____
_____
_____
_____
_____

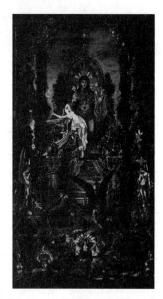

FIG. 28-24A MOREAU, Jupiter and Semele, ca. 1875.

_____
_____
_____
_____
_____
_____
_____
_____
_____

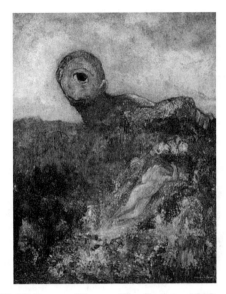

FIG. 28-25 ODILON REDON, *The Cyclops,* 1898. Oil on canvas, 2′ 1″ × 1′ 8″. Kröller-Müller Foundation, Otterlo.

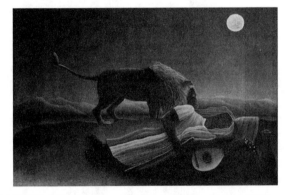

FIG. 28-26 HENRI ROUSSEAU, *Sleeping Gypsy,* 1897. Oil on canvas, 4′ 3″ × 6′ 7″. Museum of Modern Art, New York (gift of Mrs. Simon Guggenheim).

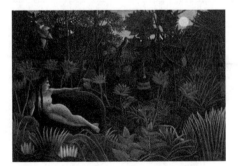

FIG. 28-26A ROUSSEAU, The Dream, 1910.

178

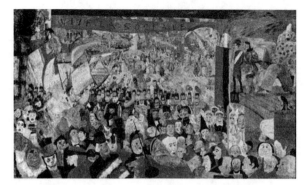

FIG. 28-27 JAMES ENSOR, Christ's Entry into Brussels in 1889, 1888. Oil on canvas, 8′ 3 1/2″ × 14′ 1 1/2″. J. Paul Getty Museum, Los Angeles.

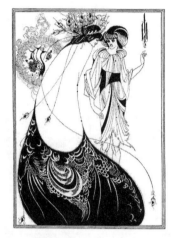

FIG. 28-27A BEARDSLEY, The Peacock Skirt, 1894.

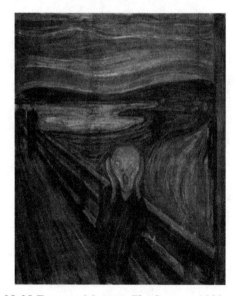

FIG. 28-28 EDVARD MUNCH, *The Scream,* 1893. Tempura and pastels on cardboard, 2′ 11 3/4″ × 2′ 5″. National Gallery, Oslo.

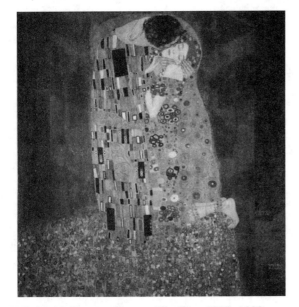

_____
_____
_____
_____
_____
_____
_____
_____
_____

FIG. 28-29 GUSTAV KLIMT, *The Kiss,* 1907–1908.
Oil on canvas, 5′ 10 3/4″ × 5′ 10 3/4″. Österreichische
Galerie Belvedere, Vienna.

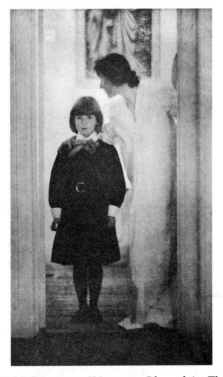

_____
_____
_____
_____
_____
_____
_____
_____
_____

FIG. 28-30 GERTRUDE KÄSEBIER, *Blessed Art Thou
among Women,* 1899. Platinum print on Japanese tissue,
9 3/8″ × 5 1/2″. Museum of Modern Art, New York
(gift of Mrs. Hermine M. Turner).

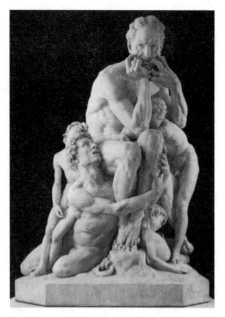

FIG. 28-31 Jean-Baptiste Carpeaux, *Ugolino and His Children,* 1865–1867. Marble, 6′ 5″ high. Metropolitan Museum of Art, New York (Josephine Bay Paul and C. Michael Paul Foundation, Inc., and the Charles Ulrich and Josephine Bay Foundation, Inc., gifts, 1967).

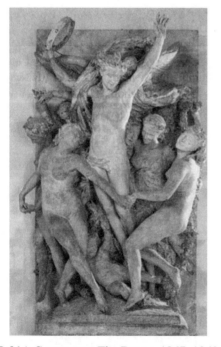

FIG. 28-31A Carpeaux, The Dance, 1867–1869.

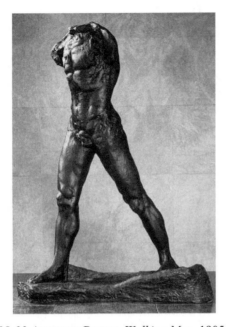

FIG. 28-32 AUGUSTE RODIN, *Walking Man,* 1905. Bronze, 6′ 11 3/4″ high. Musée d'Orsay, Paris.

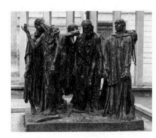

FIG. 28-32A RODIN, Burghers of Calais, 1884–1889.

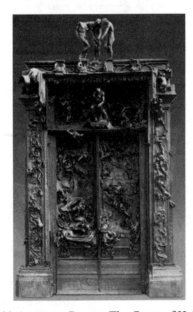

FIG. 28-33 AUGUSTE RODIN, The Gates of Hell, 1880–1900. (cast in 1917). Bronze, 20′ 10″ × 13′ 1″. Musée Rodin, Paris.

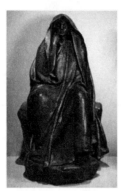

FIG. 28-33A SAINT-GAUDENS, Adams Memorial, 1886–1891.

_____
_____
_____
_____
_____
_____
_____
_____
_____

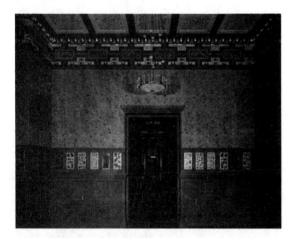

FIG. 28-34 WILLIAM MORRIS, Green Dining Room, South Kensington Museum (now Victoria & Albert Museum), London, England, 1867.

_____
_____
_____
_____
_____
_____
_____
_____

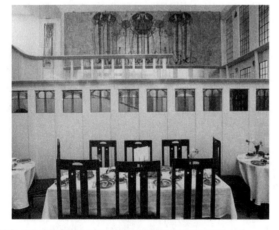

FIG. 28-35 CHARLES RENNIE MACKINTOSH and MARGARET MACDONALD MACKINTOSH, Ladies' Luncheon Room, Glasgow, Scotland, 1900–1912. Reconstructed
(1992–1995) in the Glasgow Art Galleries and Museum, Glasgow.

_____
_____
_____
_____
_____
_____
_____

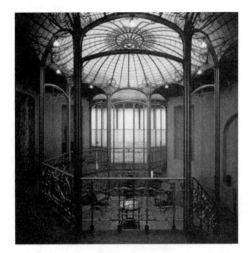

FIG. 28-36 VICTOR HORTA, staircase in the Van Eetvelde House, Brussels, 1895.

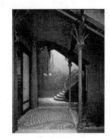

FIG. 28-36A HORTA, Tassel House, Brussels, 1892–1893.

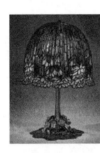

FIG. 28-36B TIFFANY, water lily lamp, 1904–1915.

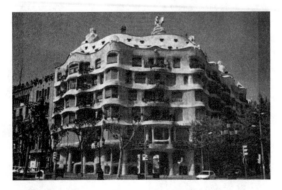

FIG. 28-37 ANTONIO GAUDI, Casa Milá, Barcelona, Spain, 1907.

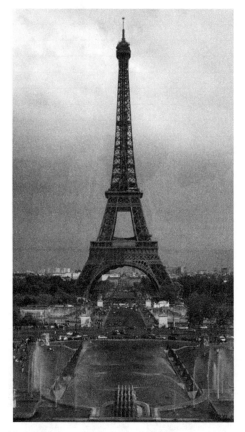

FIG. 28-38 ALEXANDRE-GUSTAVE EIFFEL, Eiffel
Tower (looking southeast), Paris, France, 1889.

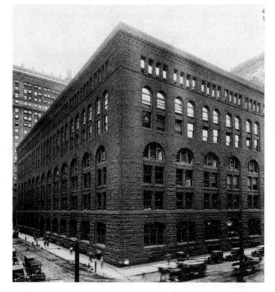

FIG. 28-39 HENRY HOBSON RICHARDSON, Marshall
Field wholesale store, Chicago, 1885–1887
(demolished 1930).

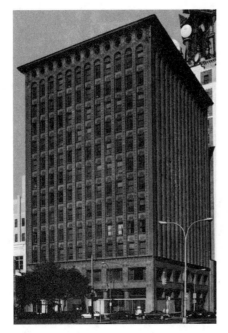

FIG. 28-40 LOUIS HENRY SULLIVAN, Guaranty
(Prudential) Building, Buffalo, New York, 1894–1896.
(page 850)

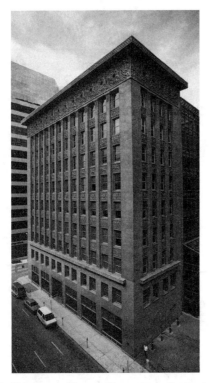

FIG. 28-40A LOUIS HENRY SULLICAN, Guaranty
(prudential) Building, Buffalo, New York, 1894–1896.

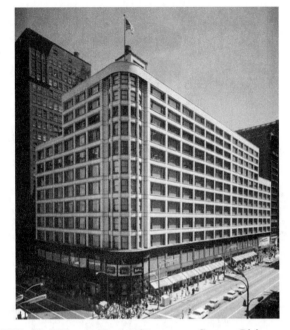

FIG. 28-41 Louis Henry Sullivan, Carson, Pirie, Scott Building, Chicago, 1899–1904. (page 850)

Chapter 29

Modernism in Europe and America, 1900 to 1945

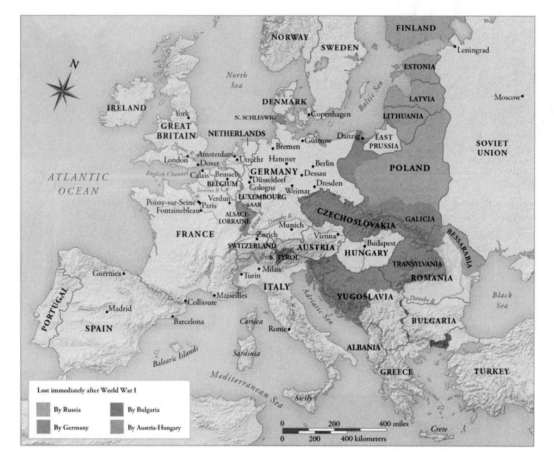

MAP 29-1 Europe at the end of World War I.

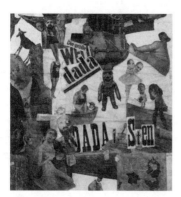

FIG. 29-01 HANNAH HOCH, Cut with the Kitch Knife Dada through the Last Weimar Beer Belly Cultural Epoch of Germany, 1919-1920. Photomontage, 3/9″ × 2/11 1/2″. Neue Nationalgalerie, Staaliche Museen zu Berlin, Berlin.

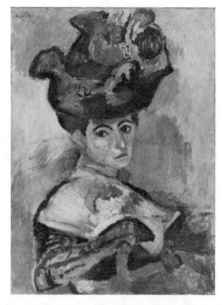

FIG. 29-02 HENRI MATISSE, *Woman with the Hat,* 1905. Oil on canvas, 2′ 7 3/4″ × 1′ 11 1/2″. San Francisco Museum of Modern Art, San Francisco (bequest of Elise S. Haas).

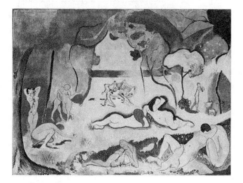

FIG. 29-02A MATISSE, Le Bonheur de, Vivre, 1905–1906.

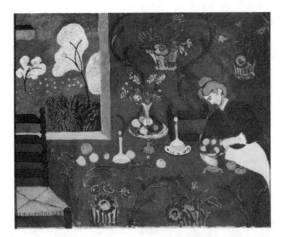

_____
_____
_____
_____
_____
_____
_____
_____

FIG. 29-03 HENRI MATISSE, *Red Room (Harmony in Red),* 1908–1909. Oil on canvas, 5′11″ × 8′1″. State Hermitage Museum, Saint Petersburg.

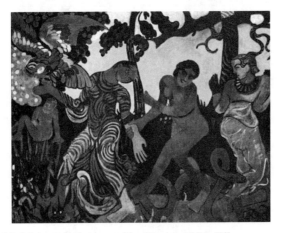

_____
_____
_____
_____
_____
_____
_____

FIG. 29-04 ANDRÉ DERAIN, *The Dance,* 1906. Oil on canvas, 6′ 7/8″ × 6′ 10 1/4″. Fridart Foundation, London.

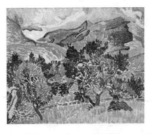

_____
_____
_____
_____
_____
_____
_____
_____

FIG. 29-04A DERAIN, Mountain at Collioure, 1905.

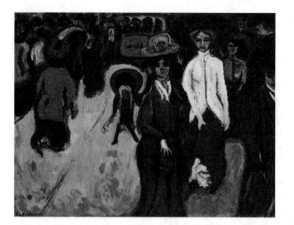

FIG. 29-05 ERNST LUDWIG KIRCHNER, *Street, Dresden,* 1908
(dated 1907). Oil on canvas, 4′ 11 1/4″ × 6′ 6 7/8″. Museum of
Modern Art, New York.

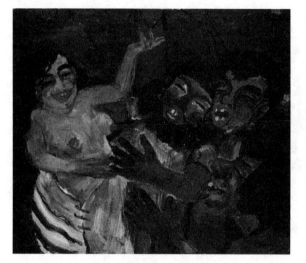

FIG. 29-06 EMIL NOLDE, *Saint Mary of Egypt among Sinners,*
1912. Left panel of a triptych, oil on canvas, 2′ 10″ × 3′ 3″.
Hamburger Kunsthalle, Hamburg.

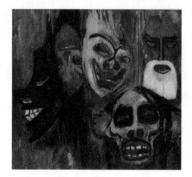

FIG. 29-06A NOLDE, Masks, 1911.

191

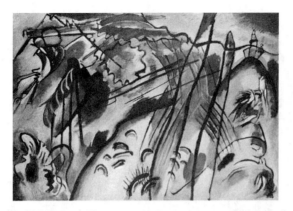

FIG. 29-07 VASSILY KANDINSKY, *Improvisation 28* (second version), 1912. Oil on canvas, 3′ 7 7/8″ × 5′ 3 7/8″. Solomon R. Guggenheim Museum, New York (gift of Solomon R. Guggenheim, 1937).

_____
_____
_____
_____
_____
_____
_____
_____

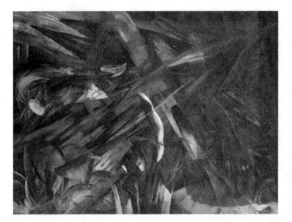

FIG. 29-08 FRANZ MARC, *Fate of the Animals,* 1913. Oil on canvas, 6′ 4 3/4″ × 8′ 9 1/2″. Kunstmuseum, Basel.

_____
_____
_____
_____
_____
_____
_____
_____

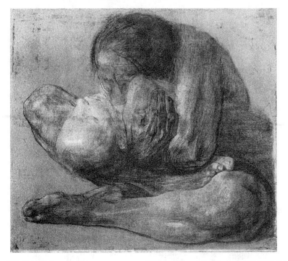

FIG. 29-09 KÄTHE KOLLOWITZ, *Woman with Dead Child,* 1903. Etching and soft-ground etching, overprinted lithographically with a gold tone plate, 1′ 4 5/8″ × 1′ 7 1/8″. British Museum, London.

_____
_____
_____
_____
_____
_____
_____
_____

192

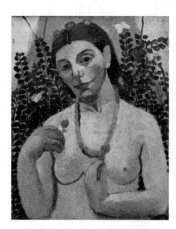

FIG. 29-09A MODERSOHN-BECKER, Self-Portrait, 1906.

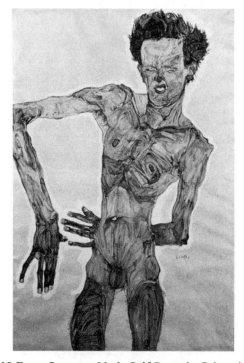

FIG. 29-10 EGON SCHIELE, Nude Self-Portrait, Grimacing, 1910. Gouache, watercolor, and pencil on paper, 1′ 10″ × 1′ 2 3/8″. Albertina, Vienna.

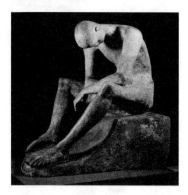

FIG. 29-10A LEHMBRUCK, Seated Youth, 1917.

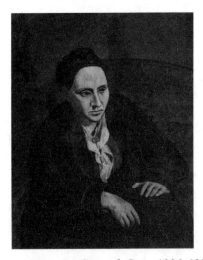

FIG. 29-11 PABLO PICASSO, *Gertrude Stein,* 1906–1907. Oil on canvas, 3′ 3 3/8″ × 2′ 8″. Metropolitan Museum of Art, New York (bequest of Gertrude Stein, 1947.)

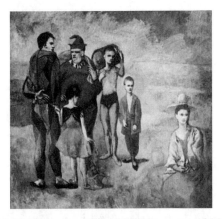

FIG. 29-11A PICASSO, family of Saltimbanques, 1905.

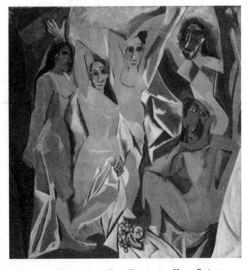

FIG. 29-12 PABLO PICASSO, *Les Demoiselles d'Avignon,* 1907. Oil on canvas, 8′ × 7′ 8″. Museum of Modern Art, New York (acquired through the Lillie P. Bliss Bequest).

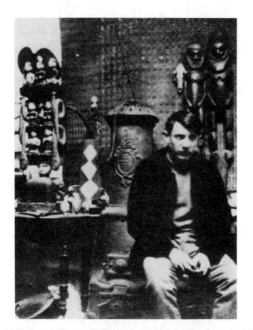

_____
_____
_____
_____
_____
_____
_____
_____

FIG. 29-13 FRANK GELETT BURGESS, Pablo Picasso in his studio, Paris France, 1908. Collection of the Musée Picasso, Paris.

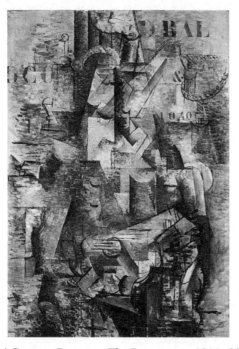

_____
_____
_____
_____
_____
_____
_____
_____

FIG. 29-14 GEORGE BRAQUE, _The Portuguese,_ 1911. Oil on canvas 3′ 10 1/8″ × 2′ 8″. Kunstmuseum, Basel (gift of Raoul La Roche, 1952).

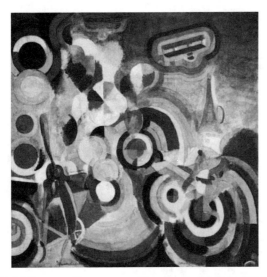

FIG. 29-15 ROBERT DELAUNAY, Homage to Bieriot, 1914. Oil on canvas, 8′2 1′2″ × 8′3″. Kunstmuseum Basel, Basel (Emanuel Hoffman Foundation).

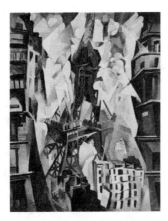

FIG. 29-15A DELAUNAY, Champs de Mars, 1911.

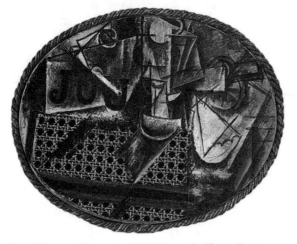

FIG. 29-16 PABLO PICASSO, *Still Life with Chair-Caning,* 1912. Oil and oilcloth on canvas. 10 5/8″ × 1′ 1 3/4″. Musée Picasso, Paris.

196

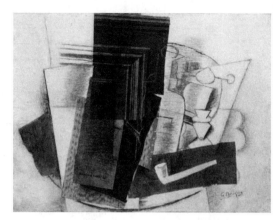

FIG. 29-17 GEORGE BRAQUE, *Bottle, Newspaper, Pipe, and Glass,* 1913. Charcoal and various papers pasted on paper, 1′ 6 7/8″ × 2′ 1 1/4″. Private collection, New York.

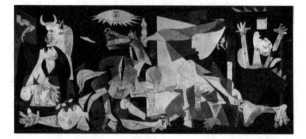

FIG. 29-18 PABLO PICASSO, Guernica, 1937. Oil on canvas, 11′5 1/2″ × 25′5 1/4″. Museo Nacional Centro de Arte reina Sofia, Madrid.

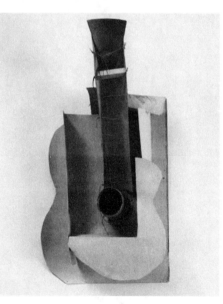

FIG. 29-19 PABLO PICASSO, maquette for *Guitar,* 1912. Cardboard string, and wire (restored), 2′ 1 1/4″ × 1′ 1″ × 7 1/2″. Museum of Modern Art, New York.

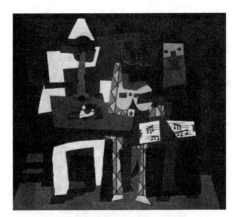

FIG. 29-19A PICASSO, Three Musicians, 1921.

_____
_____
_____
_____
_____
_____
_____
_____
_____

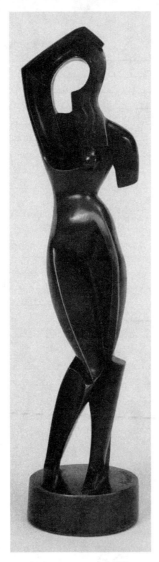

_____
_____
_____
_____
_____
_____
_____
_____

FIG. 29-20 ALEKSANDR ARCHIPENKO, _Woman Combing Her Hair,_ 1915. Bronze, 1′ 1 3/4″ × 3 1/4″ × 3 1/8″. Museum of Modern Art, New York (acquired through the Lillie P. Bliss Bequest).

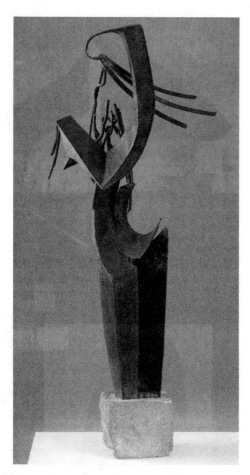

FIG. 29-21 JULIO GONZÁLEZ, *Woman Combing Her Hair,* 1936. Iron, 4′ 4″ × 1 11 1/2″ × 2′ 5/8″. Museum of Modern Art, New York (Mrs. Simon Guggenheim Fund).

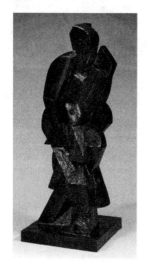

FIG. 29-21A LIPCHITZ, Bather, 1917.

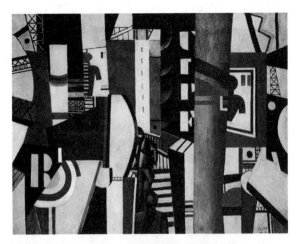

FIG. 29-22 FERNAND LÉGER, *The City,* 1919. Oil on canvas, 7′ 7″ × 9′ 9 1/2″. Philadelphia Museum of Art, Philadelphia (A. E. Gallatin Collection).

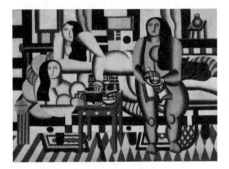

FIG. 29-22A LEGE, Three Women, 1921.

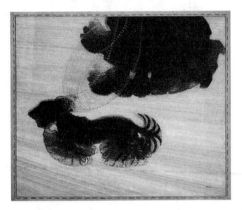

FIG. 29-23 GIACOMA BALLA, *Dynamism of a Dog on a Leash,* 1912. Oil on canvas, 2′ 11 3/8″ × 3′ 7 1/4″. Albright-Knox Art Gallery, Buffalo (bequest of A. Conger Goodyear, gift of George F. Goodyear, 1964).

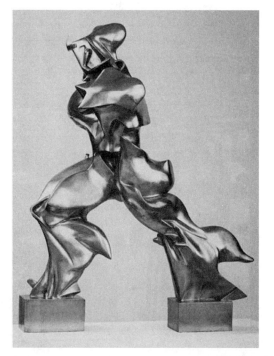

FIG. 29-24 UMBERTO BOCCIONI, *Unique Forms of Continuity in Space,* 1913 (cast 1931). Bronze, 3′ 7 7/8″ × 2′ 10 7/8″ × 1′ 3 3/4″. Museum of Modern Art, New York (acquired through the Lillie P. Bliss Bequest).

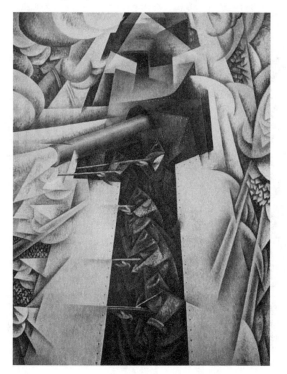

FIG. 29-25 GINO SEVERINI, *Armored Train,* 1915. Oil on canvas, 3′ 10″ × 2′ 10 1/8″. Collection of Richard S. Zeisler, New York.

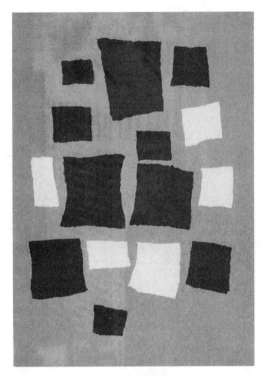

FIG. 29-26 JEAN (HANS) ARP, *Collage Arranged According to the Laws of Chance,* 1916–1917. Torn and pasted paper, 1′ 7 1/8″ × 1′ 1 5/8″. Museum of Modern Art, New York.

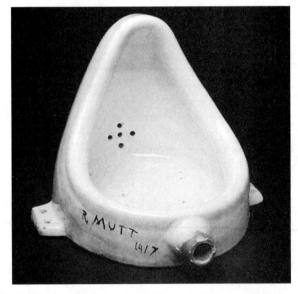

FIG. 29-27 MARCEL DUCHAMP, *Fountain* (second edition), 1950 (original version produced 1917). Readymade glazed sanitary china with black paint. 1′ high. Philadelphia Museum of Art, Philadelphia.

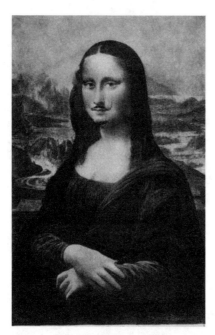

FIG. 29-27A DUCHAMP, L.H.O.O.Q., 1919.

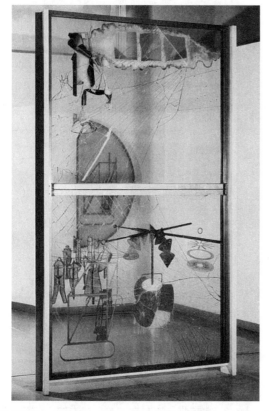

FIG. 29-28 MARCEL DUCHAMP, *The Bride Stripped Bare by Her Bachelors, Even (The Large Glass)*, 1915–1923. Oil, lead, wire, foil, dust, and varnish on glass, 9′ 1 1/2″ × 5′ 9 1/8″. Philadelphia Museum of Art, Philadelphia (Katherine S. Dreier Bequest).

203

© 2013 Cengage Learning. All Rights Reserved. May not be scanned, copied or duplicated, or posted to a publicly accessible website, in whole or in part.

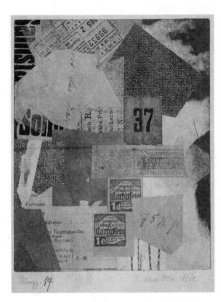

FIG. 29-29 KURT SCHWITTERS, *Merz 19,* 1920. Paper collage, 7 1/4″ × 5 7/8″. Yale University Art Gallery, New Haven (gift of Collection Société Anonyme).

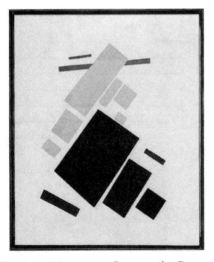

FIG. 29-30 KAZIMIR MALEVICH, Supermatist Composition: Airplane Flying, 1915 (dated 1914). OIl on canvas, 1′10 1/8″ × 1′7″. Museum o Modern Art, New York.

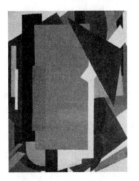

FIG. 29-30A POPOVA, Architectonic Painting, 1916–1917.

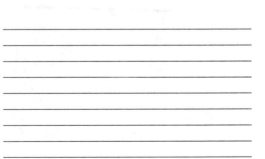
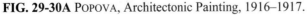

204

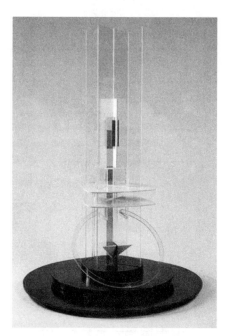

FIG. 29-31 NAUM GABO, Column, ca. 1923 (reconstructed 1937). Perspex, wood, metal, glass, 3′5″ × 2′5″. Solomon R. Guggenheim Museum, New York.

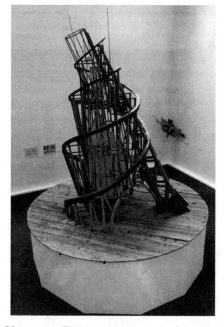

FIG. 29-32 VLADIMIR TATLIN, Monument of the Third International, 1919–1920. Reconstruction of the lost model, 1992–1992. Kunsthalle, Dusseldorf.

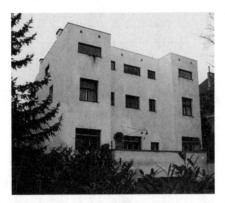

FIG. 29-33 ADOLF LOOS, garden facad of the Steiner House (looking northwest), Vienna, Austria, 1910.

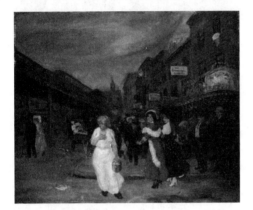

FIG. 29-34 JOHN SLOAN, Sixth Avenue and Thirtieth Street, New York City, 1907. Oil on canvas, 2′1/4″ × 2′8″. Philadelphia Museum of Art, Philadelphia (gift of Meyer P. Potamkin and Vivian O. Potamkin, 2000).

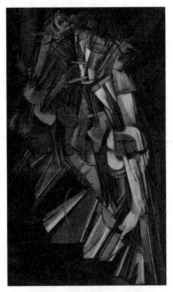

FIG. 29-35 MARCEL DUCHAMP, Nude Descending a Staircase, No. 2, 1912. Oil on canvas, 4′10″ × 2′11″. Philadelphia Museum of Art, Philadelphia (Louise and Walter Arensberg Collection).

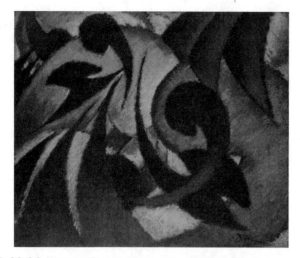

FIG. 29-36 ARTHUR DOVE, Nature Symbolized No. 2, ca. 1911. Pastel on paper, 1′6″ × 1′9 5/8″. Art Institute of Chicago, Chicago (Alfred Stieglitz Collection).

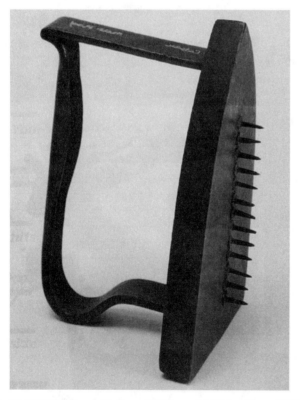

FIG. 29-37 MAN RAY, Cadeau (Gift), ca. 1958 (replica of 1921 original). Painted flatiron with row of 13 tracks with heads glued to the bottom, 6 1/8″ × 3 5/8″ × 4 1/2″. Museum of Modern Art, New York (James Trall Soby Fund).

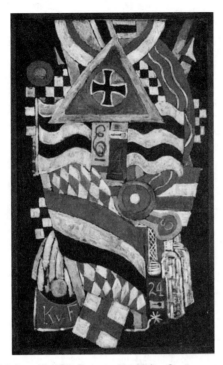

FIG. 29-38 MARSDEN HARTLEY, Portrait of a german Officer, 1914. Oil on canvas, 5′ 8 1/4″ × 3′5 3/8″. Metropolitan Museum of Art, New York (Alfred Stieglitz Collection).

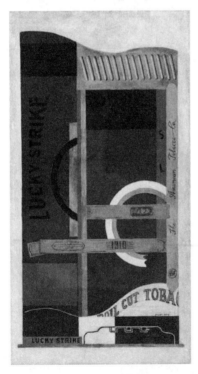

FIG. 29-39 STUART DAVIS, Lucky Strike, 1921. Oil on canvas, 2′9 1/4″ × 1′6″. Museum of Modern Art, New York (gift of the American tobacco Company, Inc) Estate of Stuart Davis/Licensed by VAGA, New York.

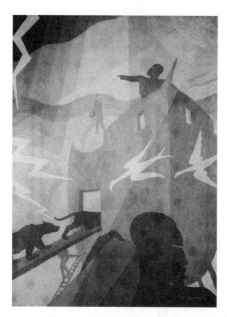

FIG. 29-40 AARON DOUGLAS, Noah's Ark, ca. 1927. Oil on Masonite, 4' × 3'. Fisk University Galleries, University of Tennesse, Nashville.

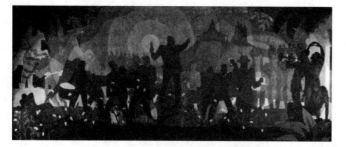

FIG. 29-40A DOUGLAS, Slavery through reconstruction, 1934.

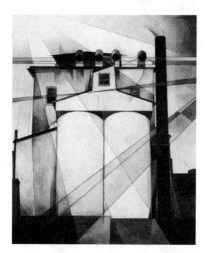

FIG. 29-41 CHARLES DEMUTH, My Egypt, 1927. Oil on composition board, 2'11 3/4" × 2'6". Whitney Museum of American Art, New York (purchased with funds from Gertrude Vanderbilt Whitney).

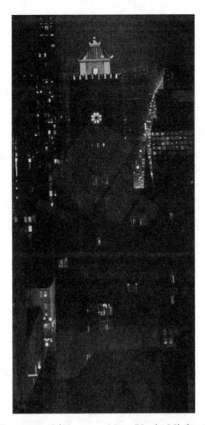

FIG. 29-42 GEORGIA O'KEEFFE, New York, Night, 1929.
Oil on canvas, 3′4 1/8 × 1′7 1/8. Sheldon Memorial Art
Gallery, LIncoln (Nebraska Art Association, Thomas C.
Woods Memorial collection).

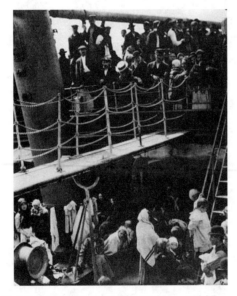

FIG. 29-43 ALFRED STIEGLITZ, The Steerage, 1907
(print 1915). Photogravure (on tissure). 1′ 3/8 × 10 1/8″. Amon
carter Museum, Fort Worth.

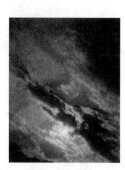

FIG. 29-43A STIEGLITZ, Equivalent, 1923.

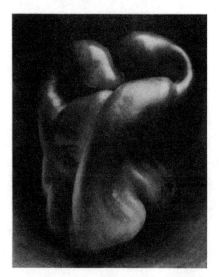

FIG. 29-44 EDWARD WESTON, Pepper No. 30, 1930. Gelatin silver print, 9 1/2″ × 7 1/2″. Center for Creative Photography, University of Arizona, Tuscon.

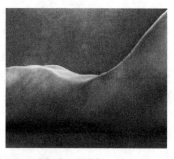

FIG. 29-44A WESTON, Nude, 1925.

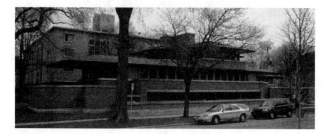

FIG. 29-45 FRANK LLOYD Wright, Robie House (looking northwest), Chicago, Illinois, 1907–1909.

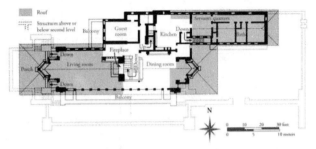

FIG. 29-46 FRANK LLOYD Wright, plan of the second (main) level of the Robie House, Chicago, Illinois, 1907–1909.

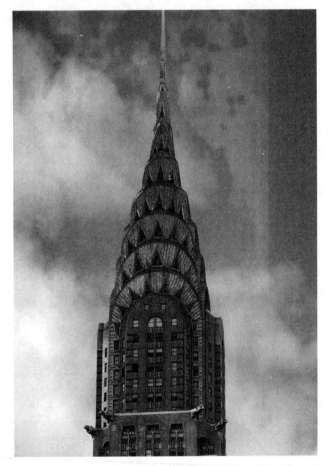

FIG. 29-47 WILLIAM VAN ALEN, Art Deco spire of the Chrysler Building looking south), New York, New York, 1928–1930.

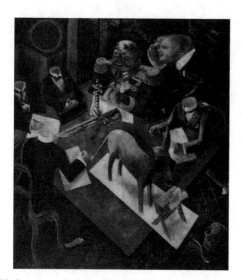

FIG. 29-48 GEORGE GROSZ, The Eclipse of the Sun, 1926. Oil on canvas, 6′9 5/8″ × 5′11 7/8″. Heckscher Museum of Art, Huntington.

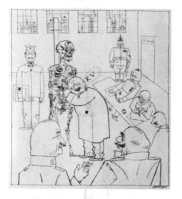

FIG. 29-48A GROSZ, Fit for Active Service, 1916–1917.

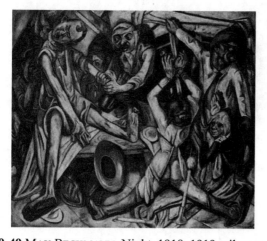

FIG. 29-49 MAX BECKMANN, Night, 1918–1919. oil on canvas, 4′4 3/8″ × 5′ 1/4″. Kunstsammlung Norhrhein-Westfalen, Dusseldorf.

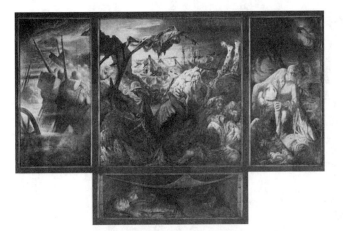

FIG. 29-50 OTTO DIX, Der Krieg (the War), 192901932. Oil and tempera on wood, 6′8 1/3 × 13′4 3/4. Staartliche Kunstammlungen, gemaldegaleria Neue Meister, Dresden.

_____
_____
_____
_____
_____
_____
_____
_____
_____
_____

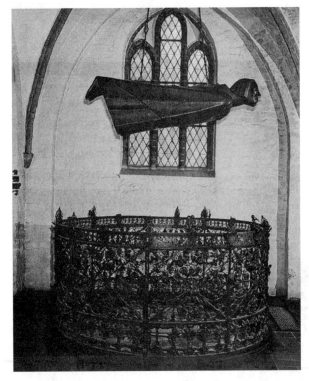

FIG. 29-51 ERNST BARLACH, War Mounument, Gustrow Cathedral, Gustrow, Germany, 1927. Bronze.

_____
_____
_____
_____
_____
_____
_____
_____
_____

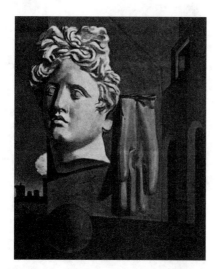

FIG. 29-52 GIORGIO DE CHIRICO, The Song of Love, 1914. Oil on canvas, 2′4 3/4″ × 1′11″3/8″. Museum of Modern Art, New York (nelson A. Rockefeller bequest).

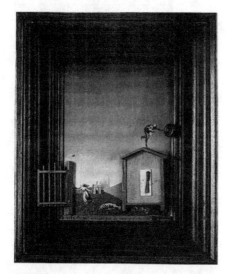

FIG. 29-53 MAX ERNST, Two Children Are Threatened by a Nightingal, 1924. Oil on wood with wood construction, 2′3 1/2″ × 1′10 1/2″ × 4 3/4″. Museum of Modern Art, New York.

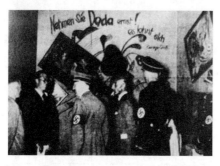
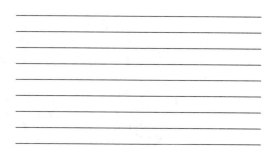

FIG. 29-54 ADOLF HITLER, accompanied by Nazi commission members, including photographer Heinrich Hoffmann, Wolfgang Willrich, Walter Hansen, and painter Adolf Ziegler, viewing the "Entartete Kunst" show on July 16, 1937.

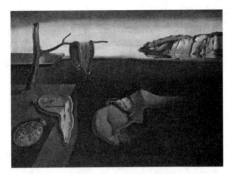

FIG. 29-55 SALVADOR DALI, the Persistence of Memory, 1931. Oil on canvas, 9 1/2″ × 1′1′. Museum of Momdern Art New York.

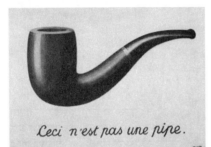

FIG. 29-56 RENE MAGRITTE, The treachery (or Perfidy) of Images, 1928–1929. Oil on canvas, 1′11 5/8″ × 3′1′″. Los Angeles County Museum of Art, Los Angeles (purchased with funds provided by the Mr. and Mrs. William Preston Harrison Collection).

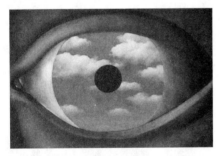

FIG. 29-56A MAGRITTE, The False Mirror, 1928.

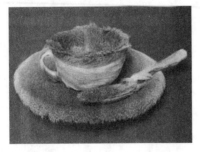

FIG. 29-57 MERET OPPENHEIM, Object (le Dejeuner en fourrere), 1936. Fur-covered cup 4 3/8″ diameter; saucer, 9 3/8″ diameter; spoon, 8″ long. Museum of Modern Art, New York.

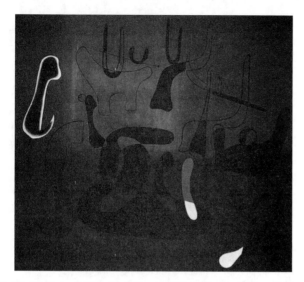

FIG. 29-58 JOAN MIRO, Painting, 1933. Oil on canvas, 5′8″ × 6′5″. Museum of Modern Art, New York (Loula D. Lasker bequest by exchange).

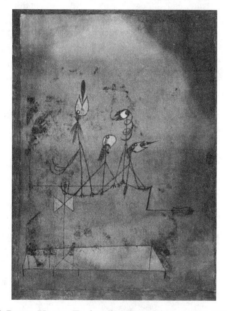

FIG. 29-59 PAUL KLEE, Twittering Machine, 1922. Watercolor and pen and ink, on oil transfer drawing on paper, mounted on cardboard, 2′1″ × 1′7″. Museum of Moder Art, New York.

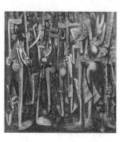

FIG. 29-59A LAM, the Jungle, 1943.

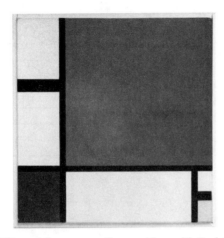

FIG. 29-60 PLET MONDRIAN, Composition with Red, Blue, and Yellow, 1930. OIl on canvas, 1′ 1/8 × 1′ 1/8″. Kunsthaus, Zurich. MondrainHoltzman Trust c/o HCR International, Warrenton, VA, USA.

_____
_____
_____
_____
_____
_____
_____
_____
_____
_____

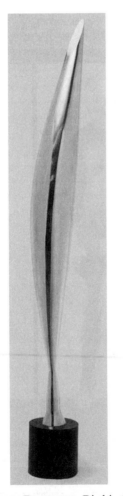

FIG. 29-61 CONSTANTIN BRANCUSI, Bird in Space, 1924,. Bronze, 4′2 5/16″ high. Philadelphia Museum of Art, Philadelphia (Louise and Walter Arensberg Collection, 1950).

_____
_____
_____
_____
_____
_____
_____
_____
_____

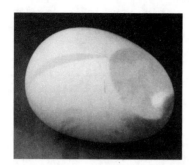

FIG. 29-61A Brancusi, The Newborn, 1915.

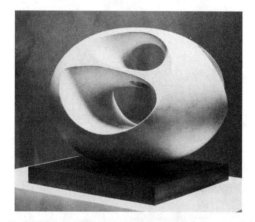

FIG. 29-62 Barbara Hepworth, Oval Sculpture (No. 2), 1943. Plaster cast, 11 1/4″ × 1′4 1/4″ × 10″. tate Modern, London.

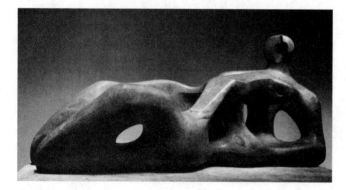

FIG. 29-63 Henry Moore, Reclining Figure, 1939, Elm wood, 3′1″ × 6′7″ × 2′6″. Detroit Institute of Arts, Detroit (Founder Society purchase with funds from the Dexter M. Ferry Jr. Trustee Corporation).

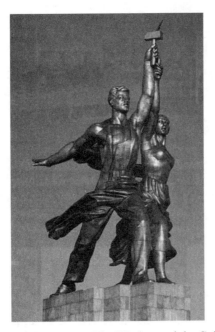

FIG. 29-64 VERA MUKHINA, The Worker and the Collective Farm Worker, Soviet Pavillion, Paris Exposition, 1937. Stainless stell, 78″ high. Estate of Vera Mukhina/ROA, Moscow/VAGA, New York.

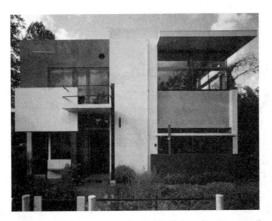

FIG. 29-65 GERRIT THOMAS Rietveld, Schroder House (looking Utrecht, the Netherlands, 1924.

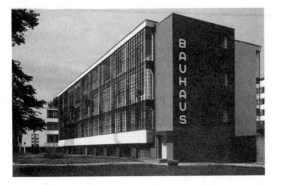

FIG. 29-66 WALTER CROPLUS, Shop Block (looking northeast), the Bauhaus, Dessau, Germany, 1925–1926.

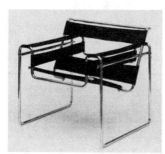

FIG. 29-66A BREUER, Wassily chair, 1925.

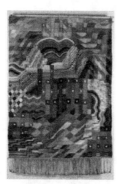

FIG. 29-66B STOLZL, Gobelin tapestry, 1927–1928.

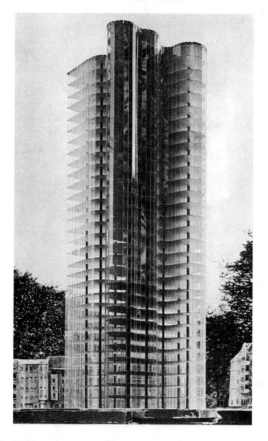

FIG. 29-67 LUDWIG Mies VAN DER ROHE, model for a glass skyscraper, Berlin, Germany, 1922 (no longer extant).

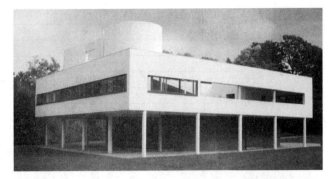

FIG. 29-68 LE CORBUSIER, Villa Savoye (looking southeast), Poissy-sur-Seine, France, 1929.

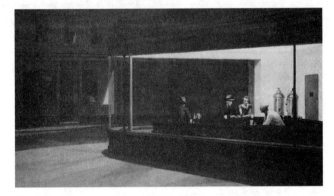

FIG. 29-69 EDWARD HOPPER, Nighthawks, 1942. Oil on canvas, 2′6″ × 4′8 11/15″. Art Institute of Chicago, Chicago (Friends of American Art Collection).

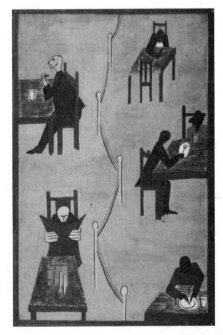

FIG. 29-70 JACOB LAWRENCE, No 49 from the Migration of the Negro, 1940–1941. Tempera on Masonite, 1′6″ × 1′. Phillips Collection, Washington, D.C.

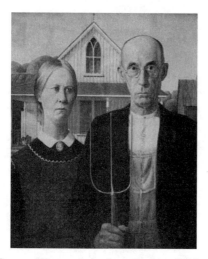

FIG. 29-71 GRANT WOOD, American Gothic, 1930. oil on beaverboard, 2′5 7/8″ × 2′7/8″. Art Institute of Chicago, Chicago (Friends of American Art Collection).

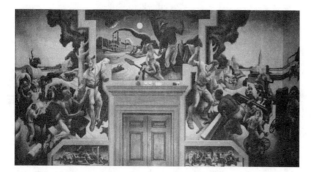

FIG. 29-72 THOMAS HART BENTON, Pioneer days and Early settlers, fresco in the State Capitol, Jefferson City, Missouri, 1936. T.H. Benton and R.P. Benton Testamentary Trusts?UMB Bank Trustee?Licensed by VAGA, New York.

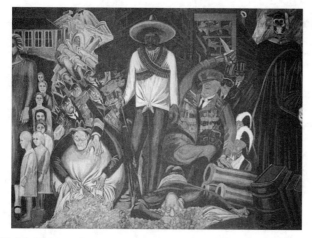

FIG. 29-73 JOSE CLEMENTE OROZCO, Epic of American Civilization: Hispano-America (panel 16), fresco in Baker Memorial Library, Dartmouth College, Hanover, New Hampshire, ca. 1932–1934.

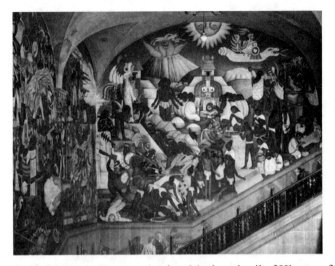

FIG. 29-74 Diego Rivera, Ancient Mexico, detail of History of Mesico, fresco in the Placio Nacional, Mexico City, 1929–1935.

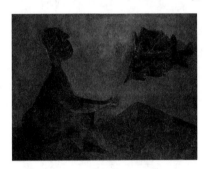

FIG. 29-74A Tamayo, Friends of the Birds, 1944.

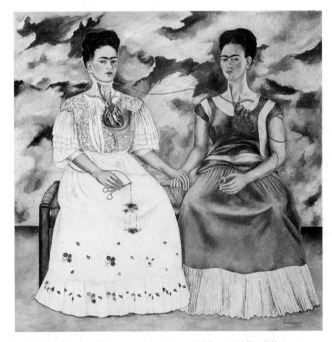

FIG. 29-75 Frida Kahlo, The Two Fridas, 1939. Oil on canvas, 5′7″ × 5′7″. Museo de Arte Moderno, Mexico City.

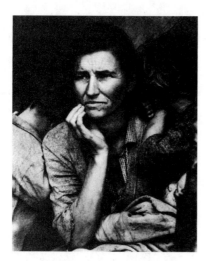

FIG. 29-76 DOROTHEA LANGE, migrant Mother, Nipomo Valley, 1935. gelatin silver print, 1′1″ × 9″. oakland Museum of California, Okland (gift of Paul S. Taylor.)

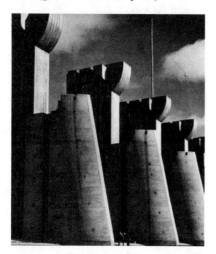

FIG. 29-77 MARGARET BOURKE-WHITE. Fort Peck Dam, Montana, 1936. Gelatin silver print, 1′1? × 10 1/2″. Metropolitan Museum of Art, New York (gift of for Motor Company and John C. Waddell, 1987.

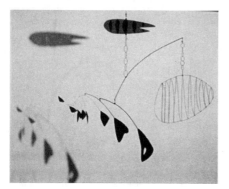

FIG. 29-78 ALEXANDER CALDER, Lobster Trap and Fish Tail, 1939. Painted sheet aluminum and steel wire, 8′6″ × 9′6″. Museum of Modern Art, New York.

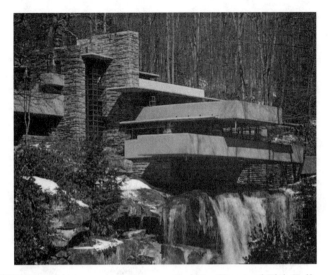

FIG. 29-79 ALEXANDER CALDER, Lobster Trap and Fish Tail, 1939. Painted sheet aluminum and steel wire, 8'6" × 9'6". Museum of Modern Art, New York.

Chapter 30

Modernism and Postmodernism in Europe and America, 1945 to 1980

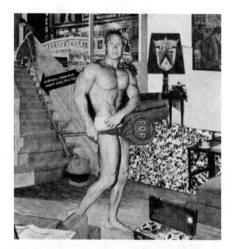

FIG. 30-01 RICHARD HAMILTON, Just What Is It That Makes Today's Home So DIfferent, So Appealing? 1956. Collage 10 3/4″ × 9 3/4″. Kunsthalle Tubingen, Tubingen.

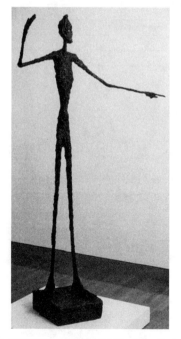

FIG. 30-02 ALBERTO GIACOMETTI, *Man Pointing* (no. 5 of 6), 1947. Bronze, 5′ 10″ × 3′ 1″ × 1 5 5/8″. Des Moines Art Center, Des Moines (Nathan Emory Coffin Collection).

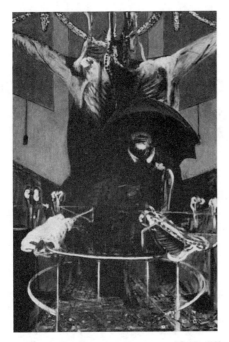

FIG. 30-03 FRANCIS BACON, *Painting,* 1946. Oil and pastel on linen, 6′ 5 7/8″ × 4′ 4″. Museum of Modern Art, New York.

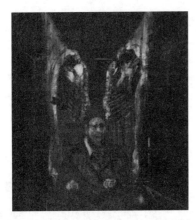

FIG. 30-03A BACON, Figure with Meat, 1954.

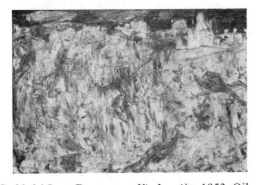

FIG. 30-04 JEAN DUBUFFET, *Vie Inquiète* 1953. Oil on canvas, 4′ 3″ × 6′ 4″. Tate Gallery, London. (gift of the artist, 1966).

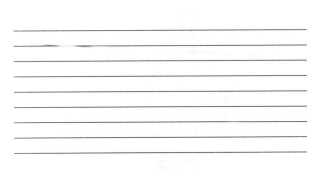

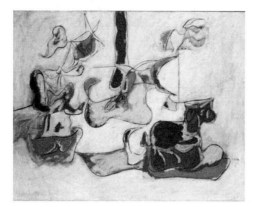

FIG. 30-05 ARSHILE GORKY, *Garden in Sochi,* ca. 1943. Oil on canvas, 2′ 7″ × 3′ 3″. Museum of Modern Art, New York (acquired through the Lillie P. Bliss Bequest).

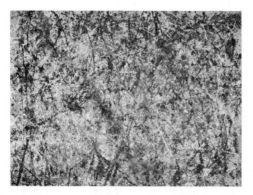

FIG. 30-06 JACKSON POLLOCK, *Number 1, 1950 (Lavender Mist),* 1950. Oil, enamel, and aluminum paint on canvas, 7′ 3″ × 9′ 10″. National Gallery of Art, Washington, D.C. (Ailsa Mellon Bruce Fund).

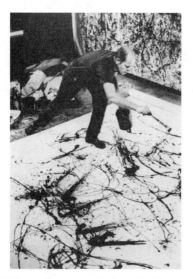

FIG. 30-07 HANS NAMUTH, Jackson Pollock painting in his studio in Springs, Long Island New York, 1950. Center for Creative Photography, University of Arizona, Tucson.

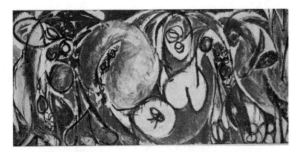

FIG. 30-07A KRASNER, The Seasons, 1957.

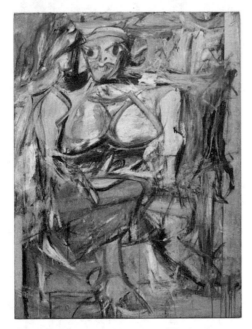

FIG. 30-08 WILLEM DE KOONING, *Woman I,*
1950–1952. Oil on canvas, 6′ 3 7/8″ × 4′ 10″.
Museum of Modern Art, New York.

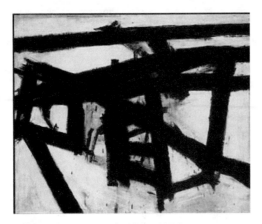

FIG. 30-08A KLINE, Mahoning, 1956.

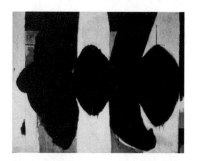

FIG. 30-08B MOTHERWELL, Elegy to the Spanish Republic, 1953–1954.

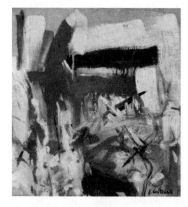

FIG. 30-08C MITCHELL, Untitled ca. 1953–1954.

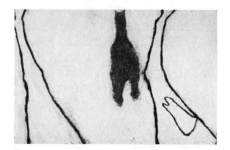

FIG. 30-08D ROTHENBERG, tattoo, 1979.

FIG. 30-09 BARNETT NEWMAN, *Vir Heroicus Sublimis,* 1950–1951. Oil on canvas, 7′ 11 3/8″ × 17′ 9 1/4″. Museum of Modern Art, New York (gift of Mr. and Mrs. Ben Heller).

FIG. 30-10 MARK ROTHKO, *No. 14,* 1960. Oil on canvas, 9′ 6″ × 8′ 9″. San Francisco Museum of Modern Art, San Francisco (Helen Crocker Russell Fund Purchase).

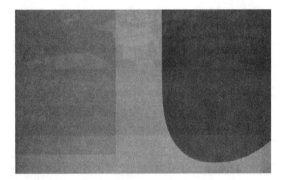

FIG. 30-11 ELLSWORTH KELLY, *Red Blue Green,* 1963. Oil on canvas, 6′ 11 5/8″ × 11′ 3 7/8″. Museum of Contemporary Art, San Diego (gift of Dr. and Mrs. Jack M. Farris).

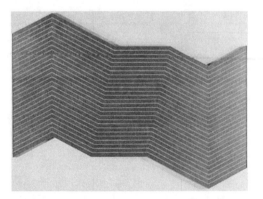

FIG. 30-12 FRANK STELLA, *Mas o Menos* 1964. Metallic powder in acrylic emulsion on canvas, 9′ 10″ × 13′ 8 1/2″. Musée National d'Art Moderne, Centre Georges Pompidou, Paris (purchase 1983 with participation of Scaler Foundation).

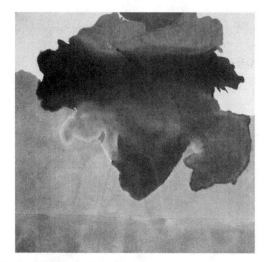

FIG. 30-13 HELEN FRANKENTHALER, *The Bay,* 1963, Acrylic on canvas, 6′ 8 7/8″ × 6′ 9 7/8″. Detroit Institute of Arts, Detroit.

FIG. 30-14 MORRIS LOUIS, *Saraband,* 1959. Acrylic resin on canvas, 8′ 5 1/8″ × 12′ 5″. Solomon R. Guggenheim Museum, New York.

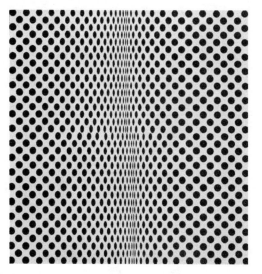
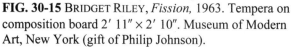

FIG. 30-15 BRIDGET RILEY, *Fission,* 1963. Tempera on composition board 2′ 11″ × 2′ 10″. Museum of Modern Art, New York (gift of Philip Johnson).

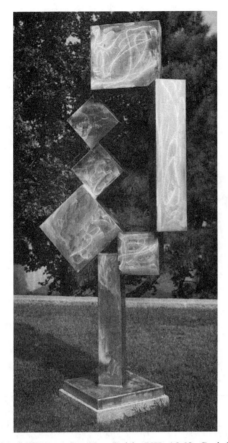

FIG. 30-16 DAVID SMITH, Cubix XII, 1963, Stainless steel, 9'1 5/8" high. Hirsh horn Museum and Sculpture Garden, Smithsonian Institution, Washington, D.C. (gift of the Joseph H. Hirsh-horn Foundation, 1972).

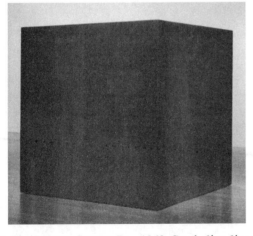

FIG. 30-17 TONY SMITH, *Die,* 1962. Steel, 6' × 6' × 6'. Museum of Modern Art, New York (gift of Jane Smith in honor of Agnes Gund).

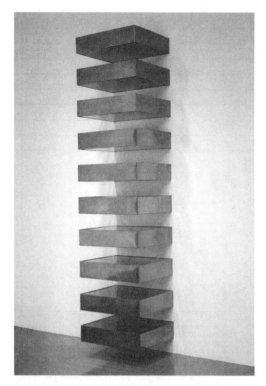

FIG. 30-18 DONALD JUDD, *Untitled,* 1969. Brass and colored fluorescent Plexiglass on steel brackets, 10 units, 6 1/8″ × 2′ × 2′ 3″ each, with 6″ intervals. Hirshhorn Museum and Sculpture Garden, Smithsonian Institution, Washington, D.C. (gift of Joseph H. Hirshhorn, 1972). Art Judd Foundation/ Licensed by VAGA, New York.

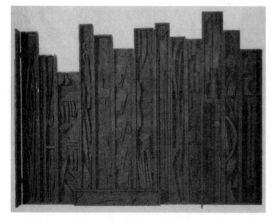

FIG. 30-19 LOUISE NEVELSON, *Tropical Garden II,* 1957–1959. Wood painted black, 5′ 11 1/2″ × 10′ 11 3/4″ × 1′. Musée National d'Art Moderne, Centre Georges Pompidou, Paris.

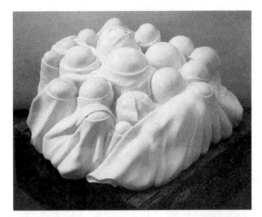

FIG. 30-20 LOUISE BOURGEOIS, *Cumul I,* 1969. Marble,
1′ 10 3/8″ × 4′ 2″ × 4′. Musée National d'Art Moderne,
Centre Georges Pompidou, Paris. Art © Louise
Bourgeois/Licensed by VAGA, New York. (page 980)

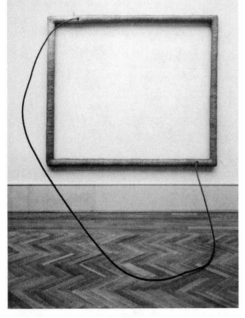

FIG. 30-21 EVA HESSE, *Hang-Up,* 1965–1966. Acrylic
on cloth over wood and steel, 6′ × 7′ × 6′ 6″. Art Institue
of Chicago, Chicago (gift of Arthur Keating and Mr. and
Mrs. Edward Morris by exchange).

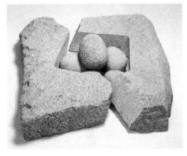

FIG. 30-21A NOGUCHI, Shodo Shima, 1978.

Chapter 30—Modernism and Postmodernism in Europe and America, 1945 to 1980

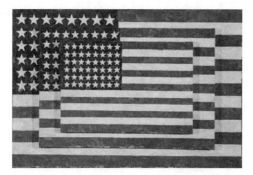

FIG. 30-22 JASPER JOHNS, *Three Flags,* 1958. Encaustic on canvas, 2′ 6 7/8″ × 3′ 9 1/2″. Whitney Museum of American Art, New York (50th Anniversary Gift of the Gilman Foundation, the Lauder Foundation, and A. Alfred Taubman).

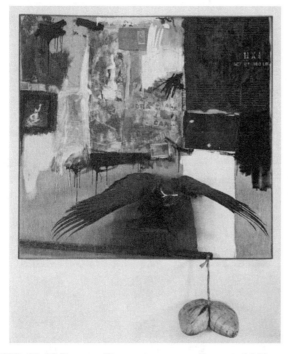

FIG. 30-23 ROBERT RAUSCHENBERG, *Canyon,* 1959. Oil, pencil, paper, fabric, metal, cardboard box, printed paper, printed reproductions, photograph, wood paint tube, and mirror on canvas, with oil on bald eagle, string, and pillow, 6′ 9 3/4″ × 5′ 10″ × 2′. Sonnabend Collection, Art © Robert Rauchenberg/ Licensed by VAGA, New York.

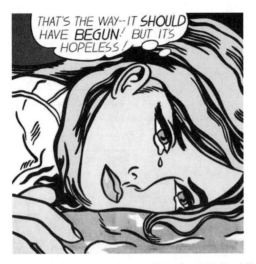

FIG. 30-24 ROY LICHTENSTEIN, *Hopeless,* 1963. Oil on canvas, 3′ 8″ × 3′ 8″. Kunstmuseum, Basel. © Estate of Roy Lichtenstein.

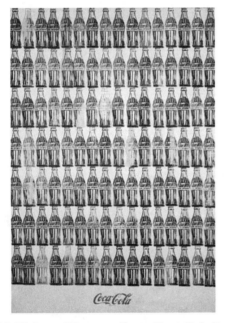

FIG. 30-25 ANDY WARHOL, *Green Coca-Cola Bottles,* 1962. Oil on canvas, 6′ 10 1/2″ × 4′ 9″. Whitney Museum of American Art, New York.

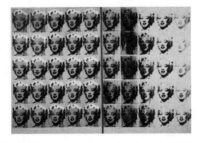

FIG. 30-25A WARHOL, Marlyn Diptych, 1962.

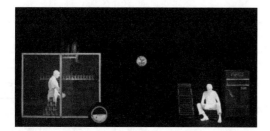

FIG. 30-25B SEGAL, Gas station, 1963.

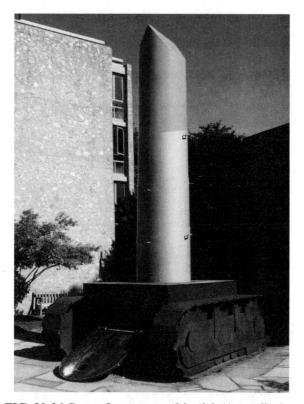

FIG. 30-26 CLAES OLDENBURG, Lipstick (Ascending) on Caterpillar Tracks, 1969; reworked, 1974. Painted steel, aluminum, and fiberglass, 21′ high. Morse College, Yale University, New Haven (gift of Colossal Keepsake Corporation).

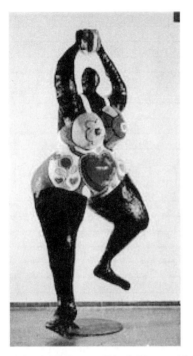

FIG. 30-26A SAINT-PHALLE, Black Venus, 1965–1967.

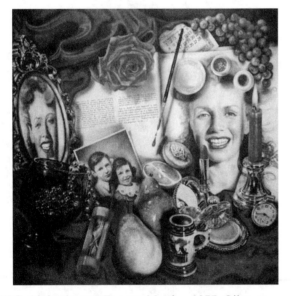

FIG. 30-27 AUDRY FLACK, *Marilyn,* 1977. Oil over acrylic on canvas, 8′ × 8′. University of Arizona Museum, Tuscon (museum purchase with funds provided by the Edward J. Gallagher Jr. Memorial Fund).

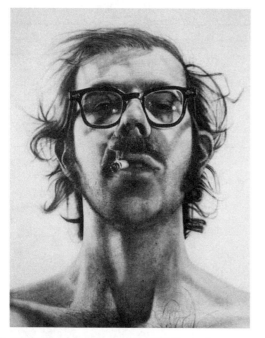

FIG. 30-28 CHUCK CLOSE, *Big Self-Portrait,*
1967–1968. Acrylic on canvas, 8′ 11″ × 6′ 11″.
Walker Art Center, Minneapolis (Art Center Acquisition
Fund, 1969).

_____

_____

_____

_____

_____

_____

_____

_____

_____

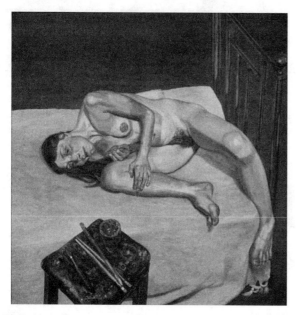

FIG. 30-29 LUCIAN FREUD, Naked Portrait, 1972–1973.
Oil on canvas, 2′ × 2′. Tate Modern, London.

_____

_____

_____

_____

_____

_____

_____

_____

_____

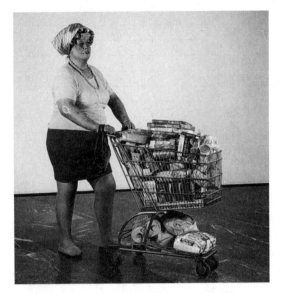

FIG. 30-30 DUANE HANSON, *Supermarket Shopper,*
1970. Polyester resin and fiberglass polychromed in
oil, with clothing, steel cart, and groceries, life-size.
Nachfolgeinstitut, Neue Galerie, Sammlung Ludwig,
Aachen. Art © Estate of Duane Hanson/Licensed by
VAGA, New York.

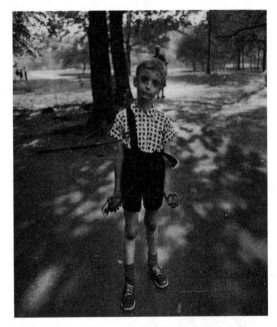

FIG. 30-31 DIANE ARBUS, Child with Toy hand
grenade in Central Park, N.Y.C., 1962. Gelatin silver
printe, 1′3 1/2″ × 1′3″. Metropolitan Museum of Art,
New York (gift of Jennifer and Joseph Duke, 2001).

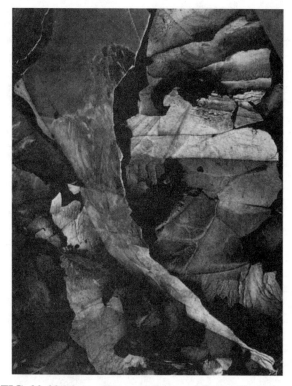

FIG. 30-32 MINOR WHITE, Moencopi Strata, Capitol reef, utah, 1962. Gelatin silver spint, 1′1/8″ × 9 1/4″. Museum of Modern Art, New York. The Minor White Archive, Princeton University.

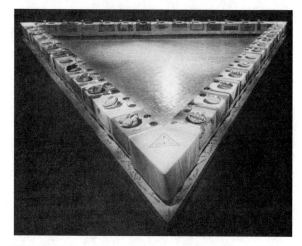

FIG. 30-33 JUDY CHICAGO, *The Dinner Party,* 1979. Multimedia, including ceramics and stitchery, 48′ × 48′ × 48′. Brooklyn Museum, Brooklyn.

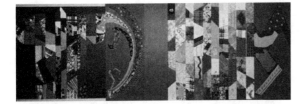

FIG. 30-34 MIRIAM SCHAPIRO, *Anatomy of a Kimono* (detail of a 10-panel composition), 1976. Fabric and acrylic on canvas, 6′ 8″ high. Collection of Bruno Bishofberger, Zurich.

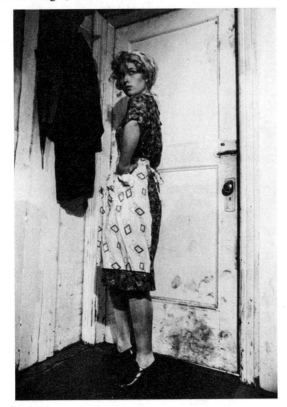

FIG. 30-35 CINDY SHERMAN, *Untitled Film Still #35,* 1979. Gelatin silverprint, 10″ × 8″. Private collection.

Chapter 30—Modernism and Postmodernism in Europe and America, 1945 to 1980

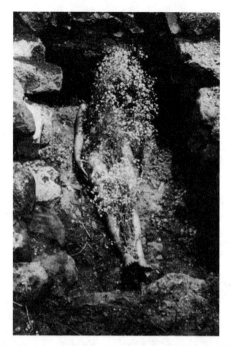

FIG. 30-36 Ana Mendieta, *Flowers on Body,* 1973. Color photograph of earth/body work with flowers, executed at El Yagul, Mexico. Courtesy of the Estate of Ana Mendieta and Galerie Lelong, New York.

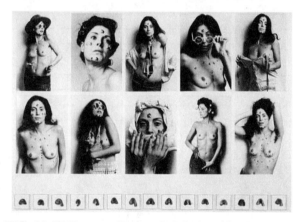

FIG. 30-37 Hannah Wilke, S.O.S. Stratification Objects Series, 1974–82. 10 black and white photographs and 16 chewing gum sculptures mounted on ragboard, 3′5″ × 4′10″ framed. Marsie, Emanuelle, Damon, and Andrew Scharlatt/Licensed by VAGA, New York, NY. Courtesy, Ronald Feldman fine Arts, New York.

© 2013 Cengage Learning. All Rights Reserved. May not be scanned, copied or duplicated, or posted to a publicly accessible website, in whole or in part.

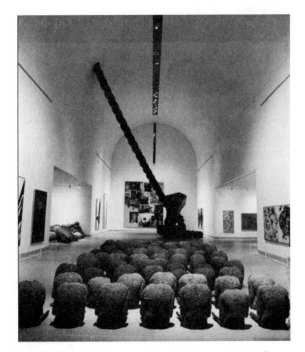

FIG. 30-38 MAGDALENA ABAKANOWICZ, *80 Backs,*
1976–1980. Burlap and resin, each 2′ 3″ high.
Museum of Modern Art, Dallas. (page 1000)

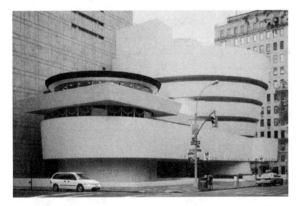

FIG. 30-39 FRANK LLOYD WRIGHT, Solomon R.
Guggenheim Museum, (looking southeast) New York,
1943–1959.

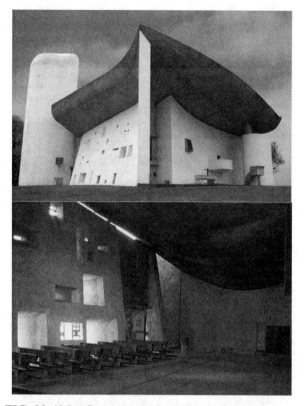

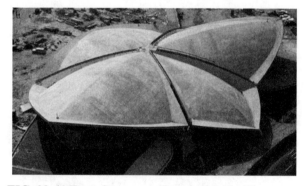

FIG. 30-40 LE CORBUSIER, Notre-Dame-du-Haut, Ronchamp, France, 1950–1955. Top: exterior looking northwest; bottom: interior looking southwest.

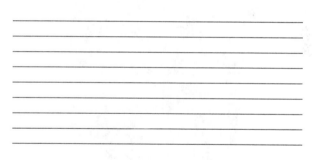

FIG. 30-41 EERO SAARINEN, Terminal 5 (Jet Blue Airways terminal, formerly the Trans World Airlines terminal; looking southeast), John F. Kennedy Internation Airport, New York, 1956–1962.

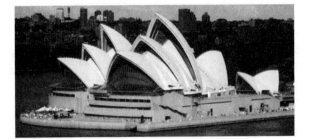

FIG. 30-42 JOERN UTZON, Sydney Opera House, (looking southeast) Sydney, Australia, 1959–1972.

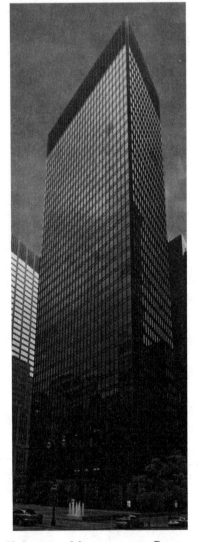

FIG. 30-43 LUDWIG MIES VAN DER ROHE and PHILIP JOHNSON, Seagram Building, New York, 1956–1958.

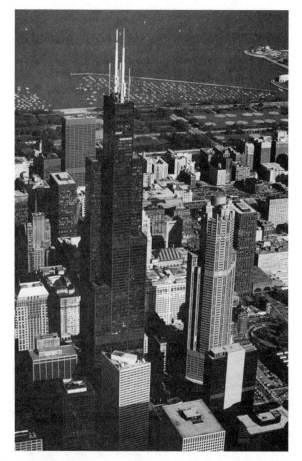

FIG. 30-44 SKIDMORE, OWINGS and MERRILL, Sears Tower, (formerly Sears Tower, looking east), Chicago, 1974.

_____
_____
_____
_____
_____
_____
_____
_____

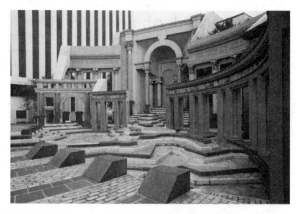

FIG. 30-45 CHARLES MOORE, Piazza d'Italia, (looking northeast) New Orleans, Louisiana, 1976–1980.

_____
_____
_____
_____
_____
_____
_____
_____
_____

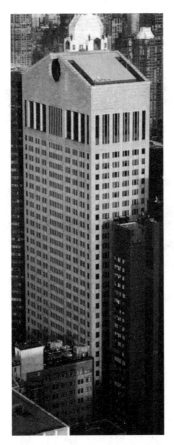

FIG. 30-46 PHILIP JOHNSON and JOHN BURGEE (with Simmons Architects), Sony Building (formerly AT&T Building; looking southwest), New York, 1978–1984.

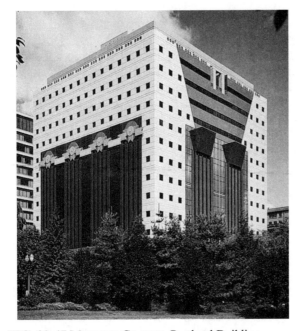

FIG. 30-47 MICHAEL GRAVES, Portland Building, (looking northwest), Portland 1980.

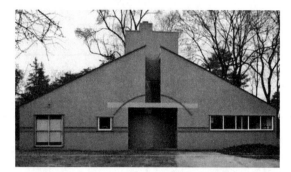

FIG. 30-48 ROBERT VENTURI, Vanna Venturi House, Chestnut Hill, Pennsylvania, 1962.

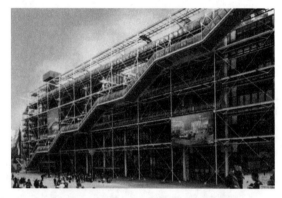

FIG. 30-49 RICHARD ROGERS and RENZO PIANO, Georges Pompidou National Center of Art and Culture (the "Beaubourg"), Paris, France, 1977.

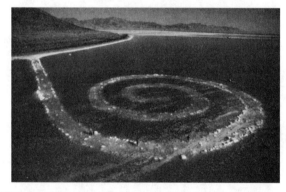

FIG. 30-50 ROBERT SMITHSON, *Spiral Jetty,* (looking northeast) Great Salt Lake, Utah, 1970. Art © Estate of Robert Smithson/Licensed by VAGA, New York.

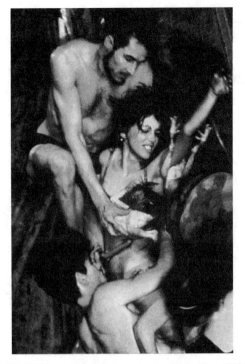

FIG. 30-51 CAROLEE SCHNEEMANN, *Meat Joy,* 1964.
Performance at Judson Church, New York City.

_____
_____
_____
_____
_____
_____
_____
_____
_____

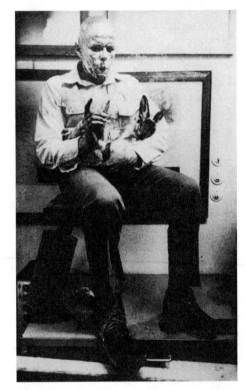

FIG. 30-52 JOSEPH BEUYS, *How to Explain Pictures
to a Dead Hare,* 1965. Performance at the Schmela
Gallery, Düsseldorf.

_____
_____
_____
_____
_____
_____
_____
_____
_____

252

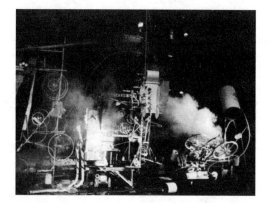

FIG. 30-53 JEAN TINGUELY, *Homage to New York,* 1960, just prior to its self-destruction in the garden of the Museum of Modern Art, New York.

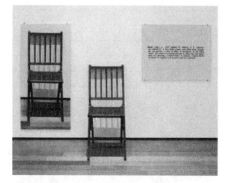

FIG. 30-54 JOSEPH KOSUTH, *One and Three Chairs,* 1965. Wooden folding chair, photographic copy of a chair, and photographic enlargement of a dictionary definition of a chair; chair 2′ 8 3/8″ × 1′ 2 7/8″ × 1′ 8 7/8″; photo panel, 3′ × 2′ 1/8″; text panel, 2′ × 2′ 1/8″. Museum of Modern Art, New York (Larry Aldrich Foundation Fund).

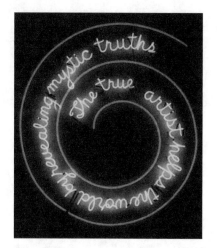

FIG. 30-55 BRUCE NAUMAN, *The True Artist Helps the World by Revealing Mystic Truths,* 1967. Neon with glass tubing suspension frame, 4′ 11″ × 4′ 7″ × 2″. Private collection.

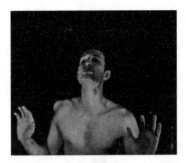

FIG. 30-55A Nauman, Self-Portrait as a Fountain, 1966–1967.

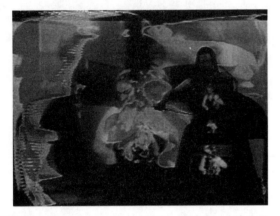

FIG. 30-56 Nam June Paik, Video still from *Global Groove,* 1973. Color videotape, sound 30 minutes. Collection of the artist.

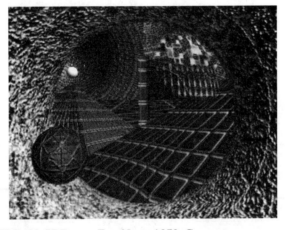

FIG. 30-57 David Em, *Nora,* 1979. Computer-generated color photograph, 1′ 5″ × 1′ 11″. Private collection.

Chapter 31

Contemporary Art Worldwide

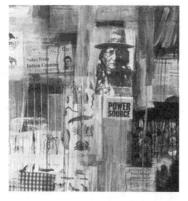

FIG. 31-01 JAUNE QUICK-TO-SEE-SMITH, *Trade (Gifts for Trading Land with White People),* 1992. Oil and mixed media on canvas, 5′ × 14′ 2.″ Chrysler Museum of Art, Norfolk.

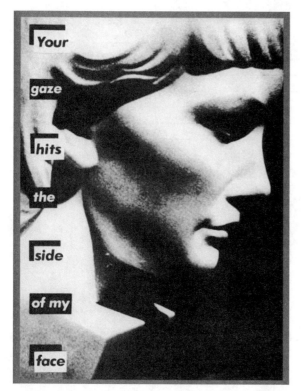

FIG. 31-02 BARBARA KRUGER, *Untitled (Your Grace Hits the Side of My Face),* 1981. Photograph, red painted frame, 4′ 7″ × 3′ 5.″ Courtesy Mary Boone Gallery, New York.

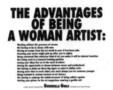

FIG. 31-02A GUERRILLA GIRLS, *Advantages of Being a Woman Artist,* 1988.

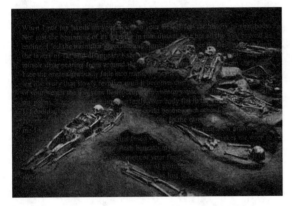

FIG. 31-03 DAVID WOJNAROWICZ, *When I Put My Hands on Your Body,* 1990. Gelatin silver print and silk-screened text on museum board, 2′ 2″ × 3′ 2.″ Private collection.

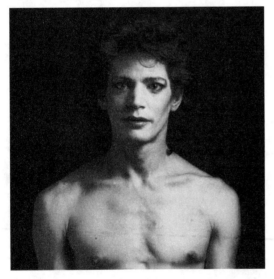

FIG. 31-04 ROBERT MAPPLETHORPE, *Self-Portrait,* 1980. Gelatin silver print, 7 ¾″ × 7 ¾″. Robert Mapplethorpe Foundation, New York.

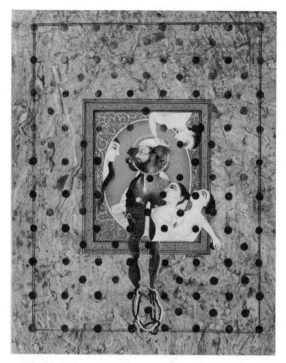

FIG. 31-05 SHAHZIA SIKANDER, *Perilous Order,*
1994–1997. Vegetable color, dry pigment, watercolor,
and tea on Wasli paper, 10 ½″ × 8″. Whitney Museum of
American Art, New York (purchase, with funds from the
Drawing Committee).

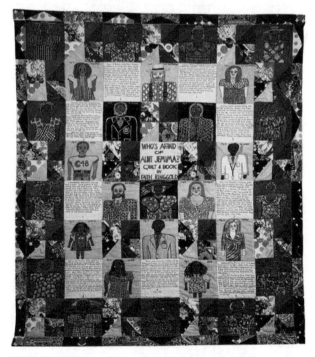

FIG. 31-06 FAITH RINGGOLD, *Who's Afraid of Aunt
Jemima?* 1983. Acrylic on canvas with fabric border,
quilted, 7′ 6″ × 6′ 8″. Private collection.

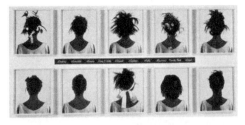

FIG. 31-06A SIMPSON, *Stereo Styles,* 1988.

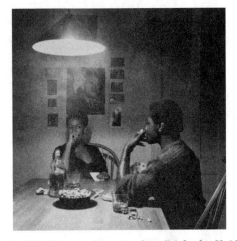

FIG. 31-06B WEEMS, *Man Smoking/Malcolm X,* 1990.

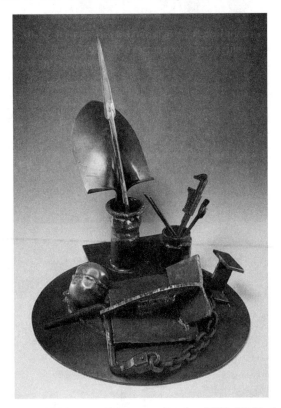

FIG. 31-07 MELVIN EDWARDS, *Tambo,* 1993. Welded steel, 2′ 4 1/8″ × 2′ 1 ¼″. Smithsonian American Art Museum, Washington, D.C.

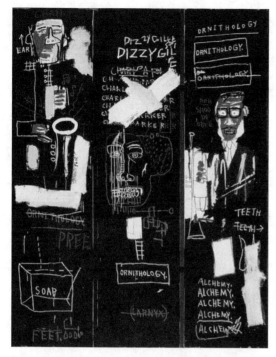

FIG. 31-08 Jᴇᴀɴ-Mɪᴄʜᴇʟ Bᴀsǫᴜɪᴀᴛ, *Horn Players,* 1983. Acrylic and oil paintstick on three canvas panels, 8′ × 6′3″. Broad Foundation, Santa Monica.

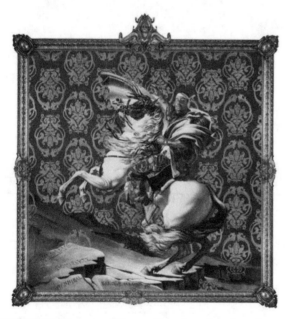

FIG. 31-09 Kᴇʜɪɴᴅᴇ Wɪʟᴇʏ, *Napoleon Leading the Army over the Alps,* 2005. Oil on canvas, 9′ × 9′. Brooklyn Museum, Brooklyn (Collection of Suzi and Andrew B. Cohen).

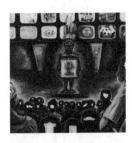

FIG. 31-09A PIULA, *Ta Tele,* 1988.

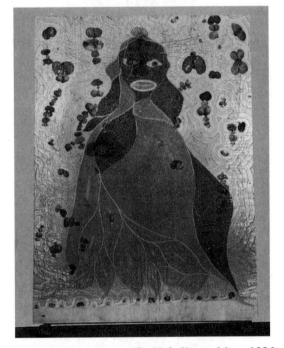

FIG. 31-10 CHRIS OFILI, *The Holy Virgin Mary,* 1996.
Paper collage, oil paint, glitter, polyester resin, map
pins, elephant dung on linen, 7′ 11″ × 5′ 11 5/8″. Saatchi
Collection, London.

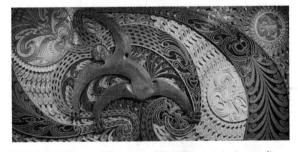

FIG. 31-11 CLIFF WHITING (Te Whanau-A-Apanui),
Tawhiri-Matea (God of the Winds), 1984. Oil on wood
and fiberboard, 6′ 4 3/8″ × 11′ 10 ¾″. Meteorological
Service of New Zealand, Wellington.

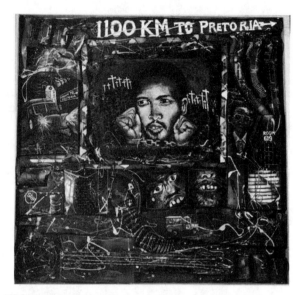

FIG. 31-12 WILLIE BESTER, *Homage to Steve Biko,*
1992. Mixed media, 3′ 7 5/8″ × 3′ 7 5/6″. Collection of
the artist.

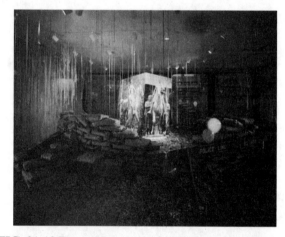

FIG. 31-13 DAVID HAMMONS, *Public Enemy,* installation
at Museum of Modern Art, New York, 1991. Photographs,
balloons, sandbags, guns, and other mixed media.

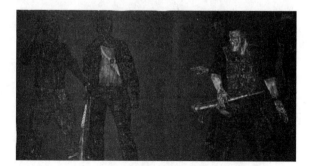

FIG. 31-14 LEON GOLUB, *Mercenaries IV,* 1980.
Acrylic on linen, 10′ × 19′ 2″. Courtesy Ronald
Feldman Fine Arts. Leon Golub/Licensed by VAGA,
New York.

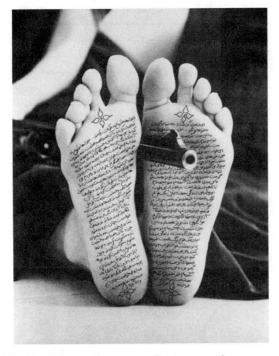

FIG. 31-15 SHIRIN NESHAT, *Allegiance and Wakefulness,* 1994. Offset print. Israel Museum, Jerusalem.

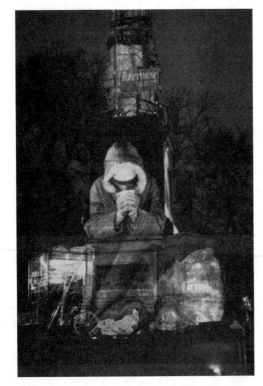

FIG. 31-16 KRZYSZT OF WODICZKO, *The Homeless Projection,* 1986. Outdoor slide projection at the Civil War Soldiers and Sailors Monument, Boston.

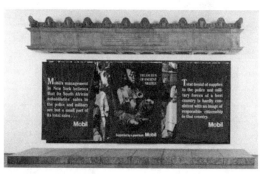

FIG. 31-17 HANS HAACKE, *MetroMobiltan,* 1985.
Fiberglass construction, three banners, and photomural,
11′ 8″ × 20′ × 5′. Musee National d′Art Moderne,
Centre Georges Pompidou, Paris.

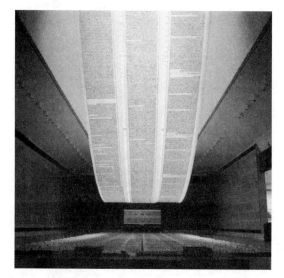

FIG. 31-18 XU BING, *A Book from the Sky,* 1987.
Installation at Chazen Museum of Art, University of
Wisconsin, Madison, 1991. Moveable-type prints and
books.

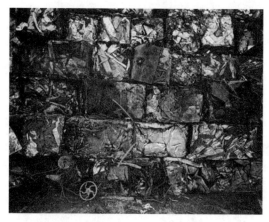

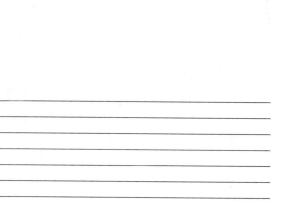

FIG. 31-19 EDWARD BURTYNSKY, *Densified Scrap
Metal #3A, Toronto, Ontario,* 1997. Dye coupler print,
2′ 2 ¾″ × 2′ 10 3/8″. National Gallery of Canada,
Ottawa (gift of the artist, 1998).

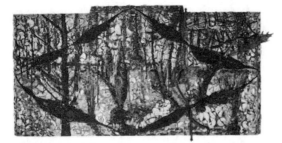

FIG. 31-20 JULIAN SCHNABEL, *The Walk Home,* 1984–1985. Oil, plates, copper, bronze, fiberglass, and Bondo on wood, 9′ 3″ × 19′ 4″. Broad Art Foundation and the Pace Gallery, New York.

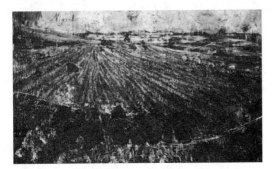

FIG. 31-21 ANSELM KIEFER, *Nigredo,* 1984. Oil paint on photosensitized fabric, acrylic emulsion, straw, shellac, relief paint on paper pulled from painted wood, 11′ × 18′. Philadelphia Museum of Art, Philadelphia (gift of Friends of the Philadelphia Museum of Art).

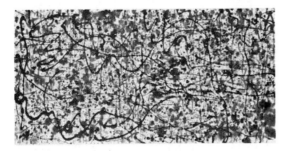

FIG. 31-22 WU GUANZHONG, *Wild Vines with Flowers Like Pearls,* 1997. Ink on paper, 2′ 11 1/2′″ × 5′ 11″. Singapore Art Museum, Singapore (donation from Wu Guanzhong).

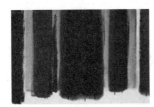

FIG. 31-22A SONG, *Summer Trees,* 1983.

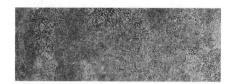

FIG. 31-22B KNGWARREYE, *Untitled,* 1992.

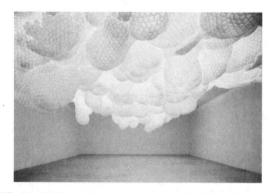

FIG. 31-23 KIMIO TSUCHIYA, *Symptom,* 1987. Branches
13′ 1 ½″ × 14′ 9 1/8″ × 3′ 11 ¼″. Installation at the
exhibition *Jeune Sculpture,* ′87, Paris 1987.

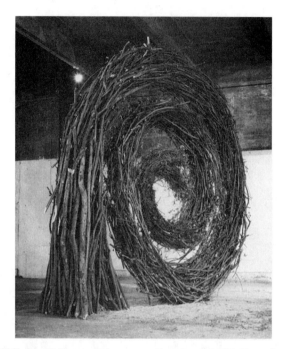

FIG. 31-24 TARA DONOVAN, *Untitled,* 2003. Styrofoam
cups and hot glue, variable dimensions. Installation at
the Ace Gallery, Los Angeles, 2005.

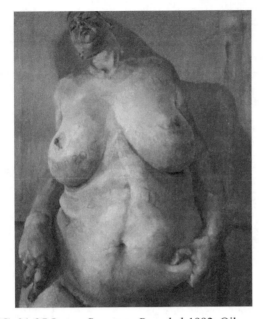

FIG. 31-25 JENNY SAVILLE, *Branded,* 1992. Oil on canvas, 7′ × 6′. Charles Saatchi Collection, London.

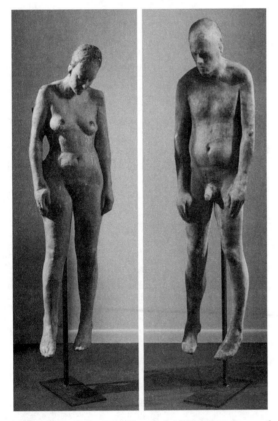

FIG. 31-26 KIKI SMITH, *Untitled,* 1990. Beeswax and microcrystalline wax figures on metal stands, female figure installed height 6′ 1 ½″ and male figure installed height 6′ 5″. Whitney Museum of American Art, New York (purchased with funds from the Painting and Sculpture Committee).

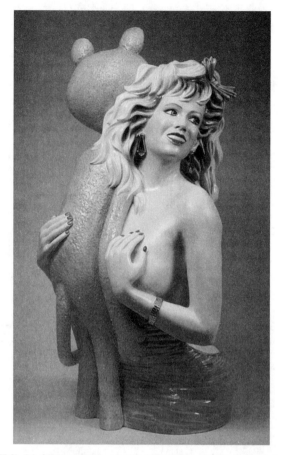

FIG. 31-27 JEFF KOONS, *Pink Panther,* 1998. Porcelain, 3′ 5″ high. Museum of Contemporary Art, Chicago (Gerald S. Elliot Collection).

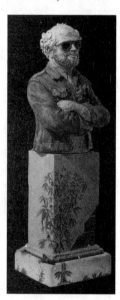

FIG. 31-27A ARNESON, *California Artist,* 1982.

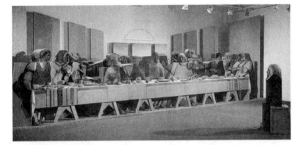

FIG. 31-28 Marisol Escobar, *Self-Portrait Looking at the Last Supper,* 1982–1984. Painted wood, stone, plaster, and aluminum, 10′ 1 ½″ × 29′ 10″ × 5′ 1″. Metropolitan Museum of Art, New York (gift of Mr. and Mrs. Roberto C. Polo, 1986).

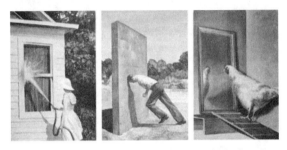

FIG. 31-28A Tansey, *A Short History of Modernist Painting,* 1982.

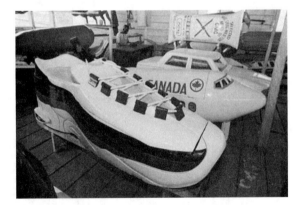

FIG. 31-29 Paa Joe, Airplane and eagle coffins outside the artist's showroom in Teshi, Ghana, 2000. Painted wood.

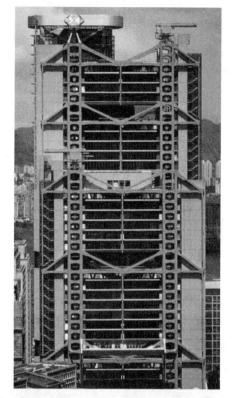

FIG. 31-30 NORMAN FOSTER, Hong Kong and Shanghai Bank (looking southwest), Hong Kong, China, 1979–1986.

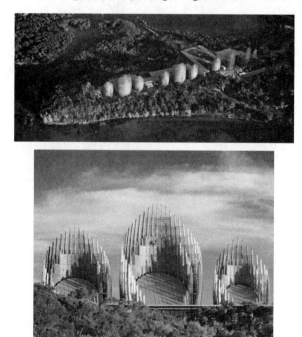

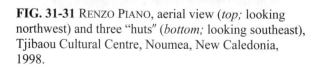

FIG. 31-31 RENZO PIANO, aerial view (*top;* looking northwest) and three "huts" (*bottom;* looking southeast), Tjibaou Cultural Centre, Noumea, New Caledonia, 1998.

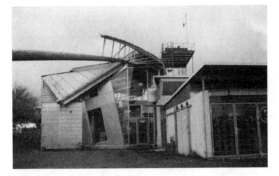

FIG. 31-32 GUNTER BEHNISCH, Hysolar Institute (looking north), University of Stuttgart, Stuttgart, Germany, 1987.

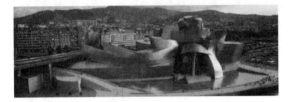

FIG. 31-33 FRANK GEHRY, Guggenheim Bilbao Museo (looking south), Bilbao, Spain, 1997.

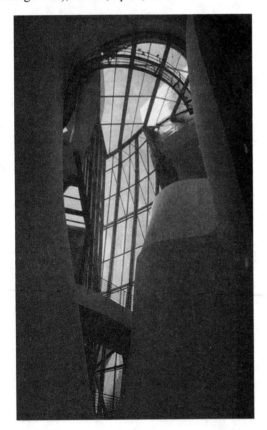

FIG. 31-34 FRANK GEHRY, atrium of the Guggenheim Bilbao Museo, Bilbao, Spain, 1997.

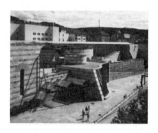

FIG. 31-34A STIRLING, Neue Staatsgalerie, Stuttgart, 1977–1983.

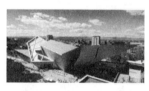

FIG. 31-34B LIBESKIND, Denver Art Museum, 2006.

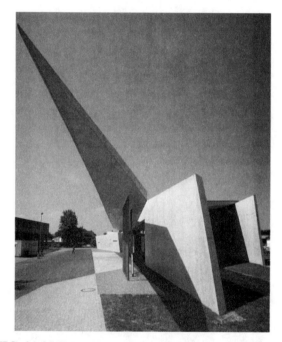

FIG. 31-35 ZAHA HADID, Vitra Fire Station (looking east), Weil-am-Rhein, Germany, 1989–1993.

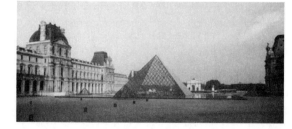

FIG. 31-36 IEOH MING PEI, Grand Louvre Pyramide (looking southwest), Musée du Louvre, Paris, France, 1988.

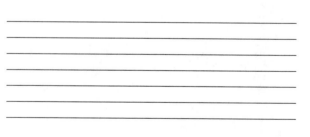

271

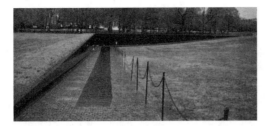

FIG. 31-37 MAYA YING LIN, Vietnam Veterans
Memorial (looking north), Washington, D.C., 1981–1983.

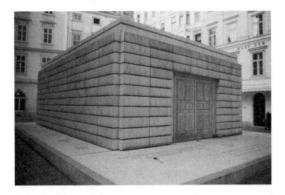

FIG. 31-38 RACHEL WHITEREAD, Holocaust Memorial
(looking northwest), Judenplatz, Vienna, Austria, 2000.

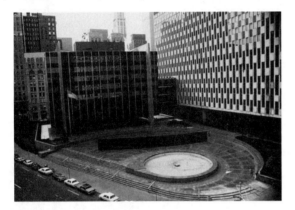

FIG. 31-39 RICHARD SERRA, *Tilted Arc,* Jacob K. Javits
Federal Plaza, New York City, 1981.

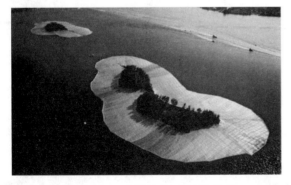

FIG. 31-40 CHRISTO and JEANNE-CLAUDE, *Surrounded
Islands, Biscayne Bay, Miami, Florida, 1980–1983.*

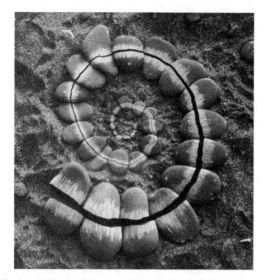

FIG. 31-41 ANDY GOLDSWORTHY, *Cracked Rock Spiral,* St. Abbs, Scotland, 1985.

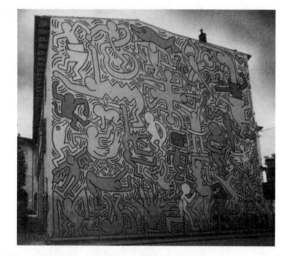

FIG. 31-42 KEITH HARING, *Tuttomondo,* Sant'Antonio (looking south), Pisa, Italy, 1989.

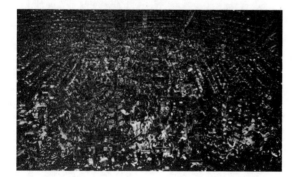

FIG. 31-43 ANDREAS GURSKY, *Chicago Board of Trade II,* 1999. C-print, 6′ 9 ½″ × 11′ 5 5/8″. Matthew Marks Gallery, New York.

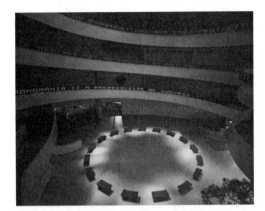

FIG. 31-44 JENNY HOLZER, *Untitled* (selection from *Truisms, Inflammatory Essays, The Living Series, The Survival Series, Under a Rock, Laments, and Child Text)*, 1989. Extended helical tricolor LED electronic display signboard, $16' \times 162' \times 6'$. Installation at the Solomon R. Guggenheim Museum, New York, December 1989–February 1990 (partial gift of the artist, 1989).

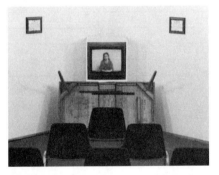

FIG. 31-45 ADRIAN PIPER, *Cornered,* 1988. Mixed-media installation of variable size; video monitor, table, and birth certificates. Museum of Contemporary Art, Chicago.

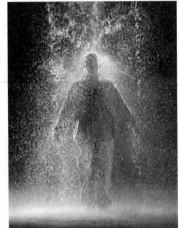

FIG. 31-46 BILL VOILA, *The Crossing,* 1996. Video/sound installation with two channels of color video projection onto screens 16′ high.

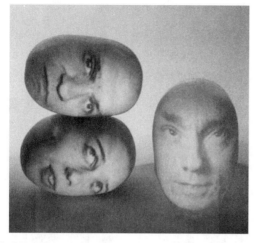

FIG. 31-47 TONY OURSLER, *Mansheshe,* 1997.
Ceramic, glass, video player, videocassette, CPJ-200
video projector, sound 11″ × 7″ × 8″ each. Courtesy of
the artist and Metro Pictures, New York.

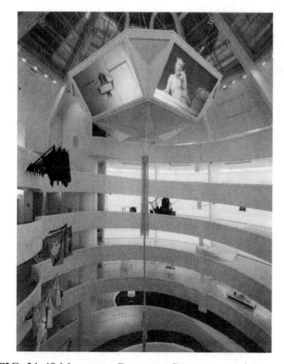

FIG. 31-48 MATTHEW BARNEY, *Cremaster* cycle,
installation at the Solomon R. Guggenheim Museum,
New York, 2003.

Chapter 32

South and Southeast Asia 1200 to 1980

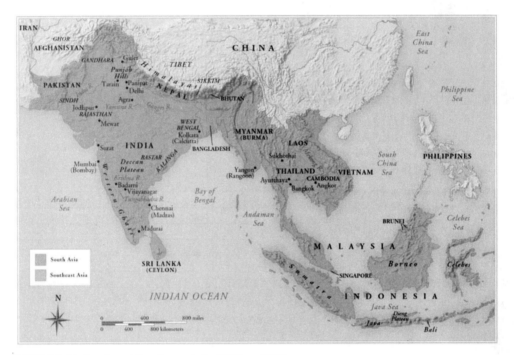

MAP 32-01 South and Southeast Asia, 1200 to 1980.

_____

_____

_____

_____

_____

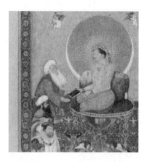

FIG. 32-01 BICHITR, JANGANGIR Preferring a Sufi Shaykh to Kings, ca. 1615–1618. Opaque watercolor on paper, 1′6 7/8″ × 1′1″. Freer Gallery of Art, Washington, D.C.

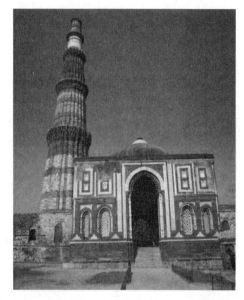

FIG. 32-02 QUB MINAR (left, looking north), begun early 13th century, and Alai darvaza (right), 1311, Delhi, India.

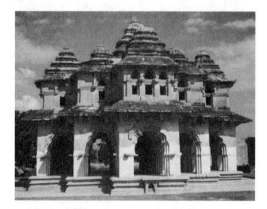

FIG. 32.03 LOTUS MAHAL, (looking southwest), Vijayanagara, India, 15th or early 16th century.

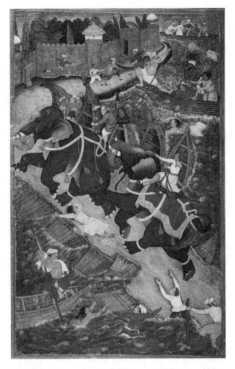

FIG. 32-04 BASAWAN and CHATAR MUNI, *Akbar and the Elephant Hawai,* folio 22 from the *Akbarnama (History of Akbar)* by Abul Fazl, ca. 1590. Opaque watercolor on paper, 1′ 1 7/8″ × 8 3/4″. Victoria and Albert Museum, London.

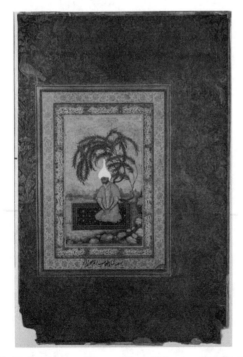

FIG. 32-05 SAHIFA BANU, Shah Tahmasp Meditating, early 17th century. Opaque watercolor on paper, figure panel 6″ × 3 5/8″. Victoria & Albert Museum, London.

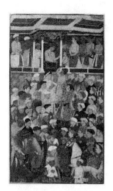

FIG 32-05A ABUL HASAN and Manohar, Darbar of Jahangir, ca. 1620.

_____
_____
_____
_____
_____
_____
_____
_____
_____

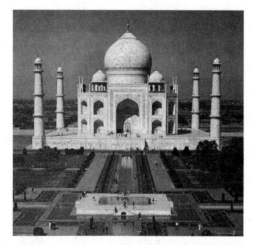

FIG. 32-06 Taj Mahal (looking north), Agra, India, 1632–1647.

_____
_____
_____
_____
_____
_____
_____
_____
_____

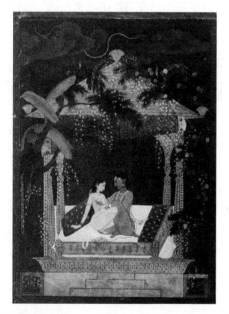

FIG. 32-07 *Krishna and Radha in a Pavilion,* ca. 1760. Opaque watercolor on paper, 11 1/8″ × 7 3/4″. National Museum, New Delhi.

_____
_____
_____
_____
_____
_____
_____
_____

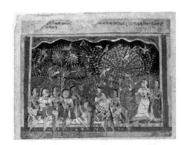

FIG 32-07A Krishna and Gopis, ca. 1550.

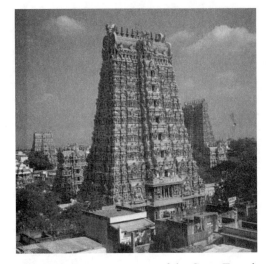

FIG. 32-08 Outermost gopuras of the Great Temple, Madurai, India, completed 17th century. (looking southeast)

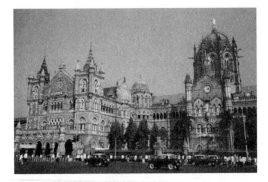

FIG. 32-09 FREDERICK W. STEVENS, Victoria terminus (now Chatrapati Shivaji Terminus; looking northeast), Mumbai (Bombay), India, 1878–1887.

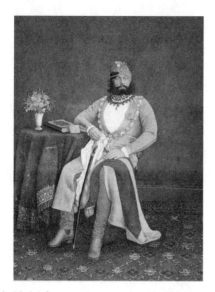

FIG. 32-10 *Maharaja Jaswant Singh of Marwar,* ca. 1880. Opaque watercolor on paper, 1′ 3 1/2″ × 11 5/8″. Brooklyn Museum, Brooklyn (gift of Mr. and Mrs. Robert L. Poster).

_____
_____
_____
_____
_____
_____
_____
_____

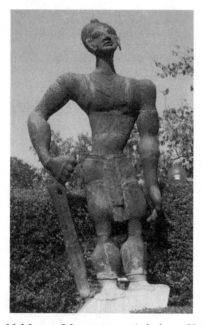

FIG. 32-11 MEERA MUKHERJEE, Ashoka at Kalinga, 1972. Bronze, 11′6 1/4″high. Maurya Sheraton Hotel, New Delhi.

_____
_____
_____
_____
_____
_____
_____
_____

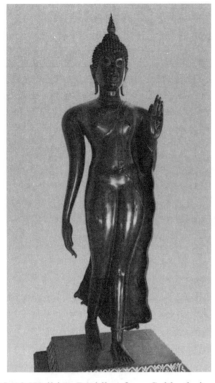

FIG. 32-12 Walking Buddha, from Sukhothai, Thailand, 14th century. Bronze, 7′ 2 1/2″ high. Wat Bechamabopit, Bangkok.

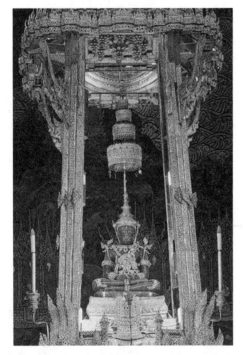

FIG. 32-13 *Emerald Buddha,* Emerald Temple, Bangkok, Thailand 15th century. Jade or jaspar, 2′ 6″ high.

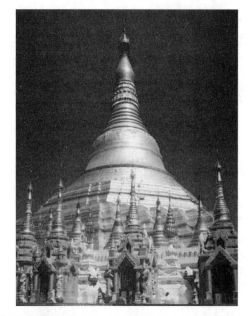

FIG. 32-14 Schwedagon Pagoda, Rangoon (Yangon), Myanmar (Burma), 14th century or earlier (rebuilt several times).

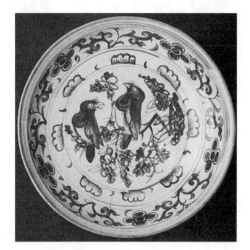

FIG. 32-15 Dish with two mynah birds on a flowering branch, from Vietnam, 16th century. Stoneware painted with underglaze cobalt, 1′ 2 1/2″ in diameter. Pacific Asia Museum, Pasadena.

Chapter 33

China and Korea 1279 to 1980

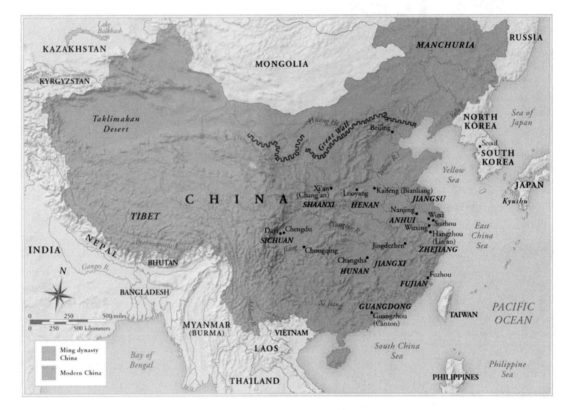

Map 33-1 China during the Ming dynasty.

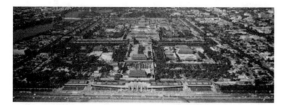

FIG. 33-01 Aerial view (looking north) of the Forbidden City, Beijing, China, Ming dynasty, 15th century and later.

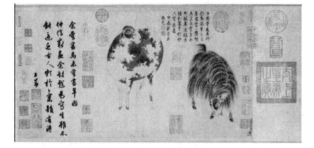

FIG. 33-01A ZHAO MENGPU, Sheep and Goat, ca. 1300.

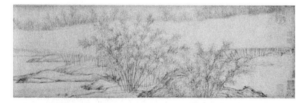

FIG. 33-02 GUAN DAOSHENG, *Bamboo Groves in Mist and Rain* (detail), Yuan dynasty, 1308. Section of a handscroll, ink on paper, 9 1/8″ × 3′ 8 7/8″. National Palace Museum, Tabei.

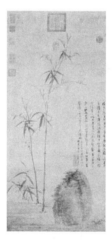

FIG. 33-03 ZHAO MENGFU, Sheep and Goat, Yuan dynasty, ca. 1300. Section of a horizontal scroll, ink on paper, 9 7/80 high. Freer Gallery of Art, Smithsonian Institution, Washington, D.C.

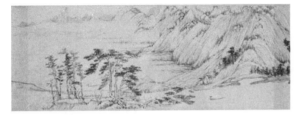

FIG. 33-04 HUANG GONGWANG, *Dwelling in the Fuchun Mountains,* Yuan dynasty, 1347–1350. Section of a handscroll, ink on paper, 1′ 7/8″ × 20′ 9″ (full scroll). National Palace Museum, Tabei.

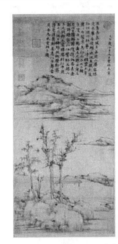

FIG. 33-04A NI ZAN, Rongxi Studio, 1372.

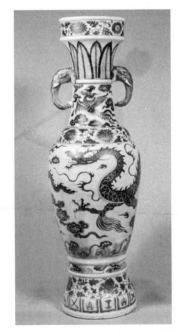

FIG. 33-05 Temple vase, Yuan dynasty, 1351. White porcelain with cobalt-blue underglaze, 2′ 1″ × 8 1/8″. Percival David Foundation of Chinese Art, London.

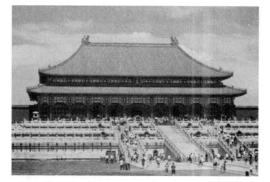

FIG. 33-06 Hall of Supreme Harmony (looking north), Forbidden City, Beijing, China, Ming Dynasty, 15th century and later.

_____
_____
_____
_____
_____
_____
_____
_____

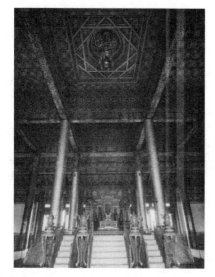

FIG. 33-07 Throne room, hall of Supreme Harmony, Forbidden City, Beijing, China, Ming dynasty, 15th century and later.

_____
_____
_____
_____
_____
_____
_____
_____

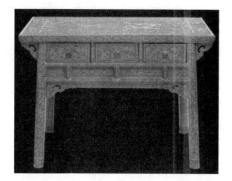

FIG. 33-08 Table with drawers, Ming dynasty, ca. 1426–1435. Carved red lacquer on a wood core, 3′ 11″ long. Victoria & Albert Museum, London.

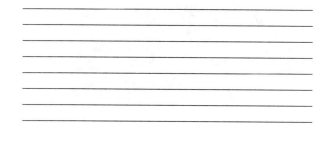

_____
_____
_____
_____
_____
_____
_____

287

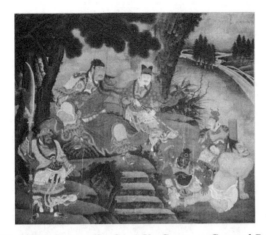

FIG. 33-09 SHANG XI, *Guan Yu Captures General Pang De,* Ming dynasty, ca. 1430. Hanging scroll, ink and colors on silk, 6′ 5″ × 7′ 7″. Palace Museum, Beijing.

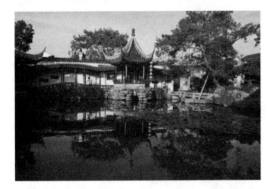

FIG. 33-10 WANGSHI YUAN (garden of the Master of the Fishing Nets), Suzhou, China, Ming dynsaty, 16th century and later.

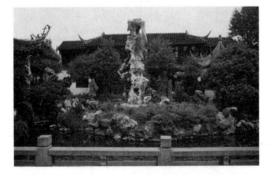

FIG 33-11 LIU YUAN (Lingering Garden), Suzhou, China, Ming dynasty, 16th century and later.

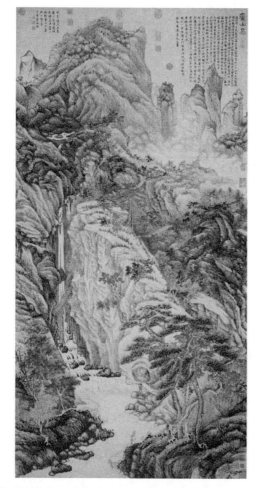

FIG. 33-12 SEN ZHOU, Lofty Mount Lu, Ming dynasty, 1476. Hanging scroll, ink and color on paper, 6′4 1/4″ × 3′2 5/8″. National Palace Museum, tabei.

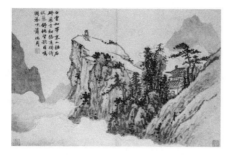

FIG. 33-12A SHEN ZHOU, Poet on a Mountaintop, ca. 1490–1500.

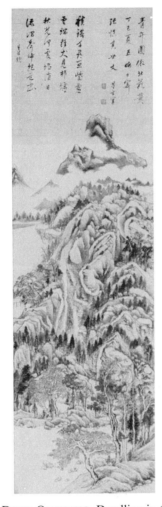

FIG. 33-13 Dong Quchang, Dwelling in the Quinbian Mountains, Ming dynasty, 1617. hanging scroll, ink on paper, 7'3 1/2" × 2'2 1/2". Cleveland Museum of Art, Cleveland (Leonard C. Hanna Jr. bequest).

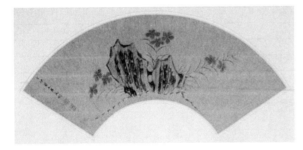

FIG. 33-14 Wen Shu, Carnations and Garden Rock, Ming Dynast, 1627, Fan, ink and colors on gold paper, 6 3/4" × 1'9 1/4". Honolulu Academy of Arts, Honolulu (gift of Mr. Robert Allerton).

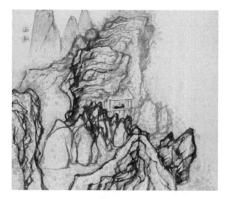

FIG. 33-15 SHITAO, Man in a house beneath a Cliff, Quing dynasty, late 17th century. Album leaf, ink and colors on paper, 9 1/2″ × 11′. C.C. Wang Collection, New York.

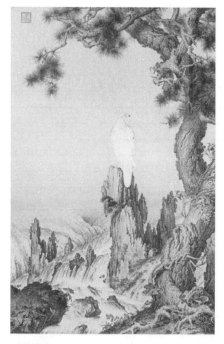

FIG. 33-16 GIUSEPPE CASTIGLIONE (Lang Shining), Auspicious Objects, Quing dynasty, 1724. Hanging scroll, ink and colors on silk, 7′ 11 3/8″ × 5′1 7/8″. Palace Museum, Beijing.

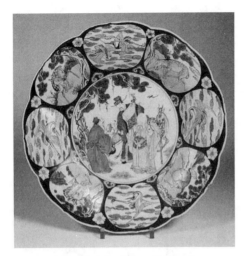

FIG. 33-17 Dish with lobed rim, Quing dynasty, ca. 1700. White porcelain with multicolored overglaze, 1′1 5/8″ diameter. Percival david Foundation of Chinese Art, London.

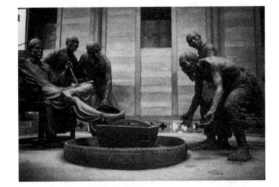

FIG. 33-18 YE YUSHAN and others, Rent Collection Courtyard (detail of larger tableau), Dayi, China, 1965. Clay 100 yards long with life-size figures.

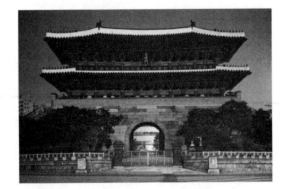

FIG. 33-19 NAMDAEMUN, Seoul, South Korea, Choson dynasty, first built in 1398.

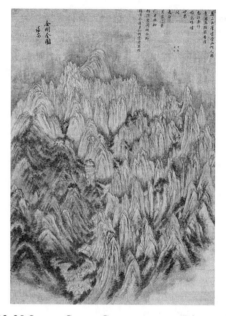

FIG. 33-20 JEONG SEON, Geumgangsan (Diamond) Mountains, Joseon dynasty, 1734.

_____
_____
_____
_____
_____
_____
_____
_____
_____

Chapter 34

Japan, 1336 to 1980

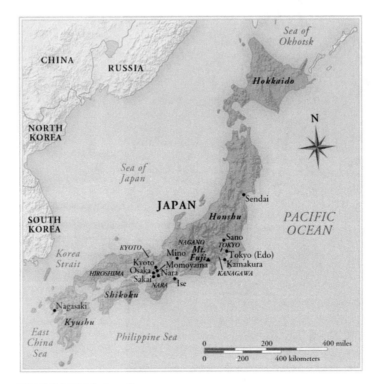

MAP 34-01 Modern Japan.

_____

_____

_____

_____

_____

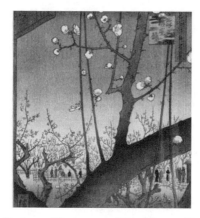

FIG. 34-01 ANDO HIROSHIGE, Plum Estate, Kameido, from One Hundred Famous Views of Edo, Edo period, 1857. Woodblock print, ink and color on paper, 1′1 1/4″ × 8 5/8″. Brooklyn Museum, Brooklyn (gift of Anna Ferris).

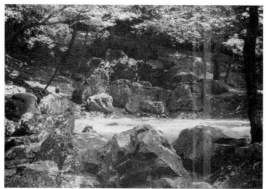

FIG. 34-02 Dry Cascade and pools, upper garden, Saihoji temple, Kyoto, Japan, modified in Muromachi period 14th century.

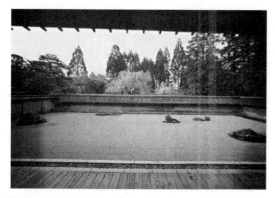

FIG. 34-02A Karesansui garden, Royoanji, Kyoto, ca. 1488.

295

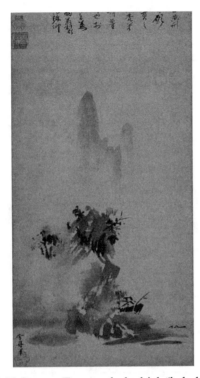

FIG. 34-03 SESSHU TOYO, splashed-ink (haboku) landscape, detail of the lower part of a hanging scroll, Muromachi period 1495. Ink on paper, full scroll 4′ 10 1/4″ × 1′ 7/8″; detail 4′ 1/2″ high. Tokyo National Museum, Tokyo.

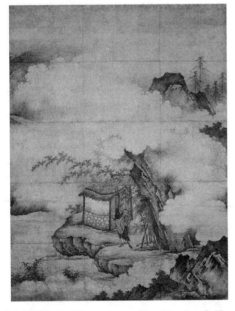

FIG. 34-04 KANO MOTONOBU, *Zen Patriarch Xiangyen Zhixian Sweeping with a Broom,* from Daitokuji, Kyoto, Japan, Muromachi period ca 1513. Hanging scroll, ink and color on paper, 5′ 7 3/8″ × 2′ 10 3/4″. Tokyo National Museum, Tokyo. (page 738)

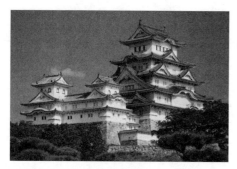

FIG. 34-04A WHITE HERON castle, himeji, begun 1581.

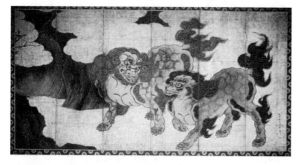

FIG. 34-05 KANO EITOKU, *Chinese Lions,* Momoyama period late 16th century. Six-panel screen, color, ink, and gold leaf on paper, 7′ 4″ × 14′ 10″. Imperial Household Agency, Tokyo.

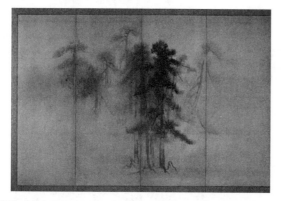

FIG. 34-06 HASEGAWA TOHAKU, *Pine Forest,* Momoyama period, late 16th century. One of a pair of six-panel screens, ink on paper, 5′ 1 3/8″ × 11′ 4″. Tokyo National Museum, Tokyo.

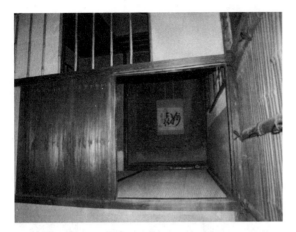

FIG. 34-07 SEN NO RIKYU, Taian teahouse
Myokian Temple, Kyoto, Japan, Momoyama period,
ca. 1582.

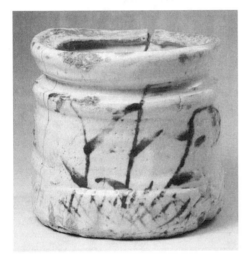

FIG. 34-08 Kogan, tea ceremony water jar, Momoyama
period, late 16th century. Shino ware with underglaze
design, 7″ high. Hatakeyama Memorial Museum,
Tokyo.

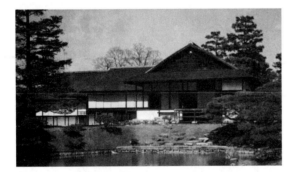

FIG. 34-09 Eastern facade of the Katsura Imperial
Villa, Kyoto, Japan, Edo period, 1620–1663.

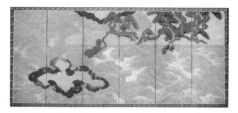

FIG. 34-09A SOTATSU, Waves at Matsushuma, ca. 1630.

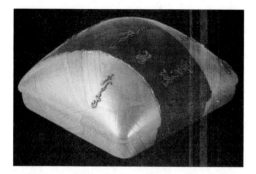

FIG. 34-10 HONAMI KOETSU, *Boat Bridge,* writing box, Edo period, early 17th century. Lacquered wood with sprinkled gold and lead overlay, 9 1/2″ × 9″ × 4 3/8″. Tokyo National Museum, Tokyo.

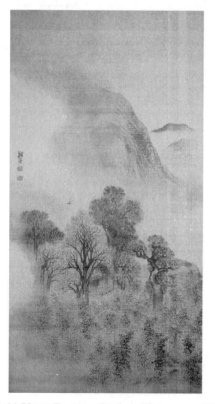

FIG. 34-11 YOSA BUSON, *Cuckoo Flying over New Verdure,* Edo period late 18th century. Hanging scroll, ink and color on silk, 5′ 1/2″ × 2′ 7 1/4″. Hiraki Ukiyo-e Museum, Yokohama.

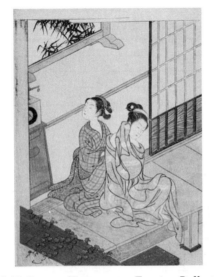

FIG. 34-12 Suzuki Harunobu, *Evening Bell at the Clock,* from *Eight Views of the Parlor,* Edo period ca. 1765. Woodblock print, 11 1/4″ × 8 1/2″. Art Institute of Chicago, Chicago (Clarence Buckingham Collection).

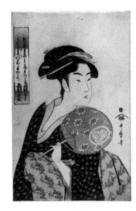

FIG. 34-12A Utamaro, Ohisa of the takashima Tea Shop, 1792–1793.

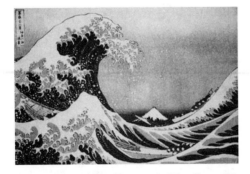

FIG. 34-13 Katsushika Hokusai, *The Great Wave off Kanagawa,* from *Thirty-six Views of Mount Fuji,* Edo period ca 1826–1833. Woodblock print, ink and colors on paper, 9 7/8″ × 1′ 2 3/4″. Museum of Fine Arts, Boston (Bigelow Collection).

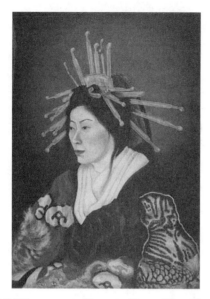

FIG. 34-14 TAKAHASHI YUICHI, *Oiran (Grand Courtesan),* Meiji period, 1872. Oil on canvas, 2′ 6 1/2″ × 1′ 9 5/8″. Tokyo National University of Fine Arts and Music, Tokyo.

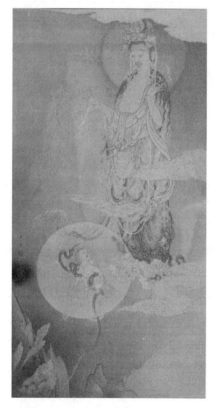

FIG. 34-15 KANO HOGAI, BODHISATTVA KANNON, Hanging scroll, ink, color, and gold on silk, 5′4 3/4″ × 2′9 3/8″. Freer gallery of Art, Smithsonian Institute, Washington, D.C. (gift of Charles Lang Freer.)

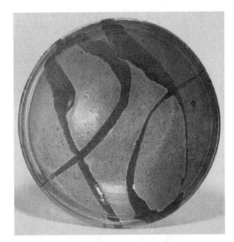

FIG. 34-16 HAMADA SHOJI, dish, Showa period, 1962. Black trails on translucent glaze, 1′ 10 1/2″ diameter. National Museum of Modern Art, Kyoto.

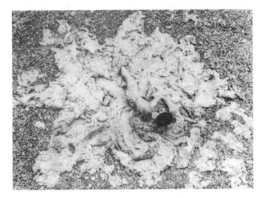

FIG. 34-17 KAZUO SHIRAGA, Making a Work with His Own Body, Showa period, 1955, Mud.

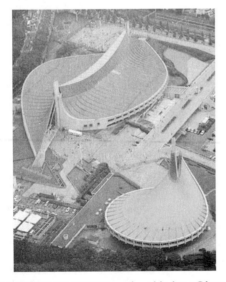

FIG. 34-18 KENZO TANGE, national indoor Olympic stadiums (looking east), Tokyo, Japan, Showa period, 1961–1964.

Chapter 35

Native Arts of the Americas 1300 to 1980

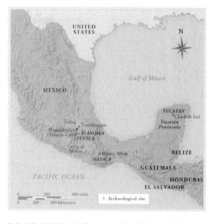

MAP 35-01 Mixteca-Puebla and Aztec sites in Mesoamerica.

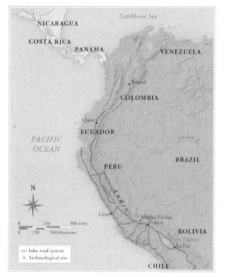

MAP 35-02 Inka sites in Andean South America.

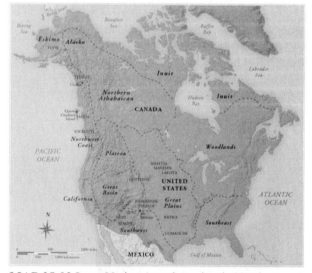

MAP 35-03 Later Native American sites in North America.

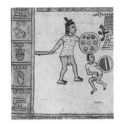

FIG. 35-01 The founding of Tenochtitlan, folio 2 recto of the Codex Mendoza, from Mexico City, Mexico, Aztec, ca. 1540–1542. Ink and color on paper, 1′ 7/8″ × 8 5/8″. Bodleian Library, Oxford University, Oxford.

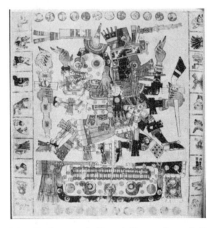

FIG. 35-02 Mictlantecuhtli and Quetzalcoatl, from the *Borgia Codex,* Mixteca-Puebla, possibly from the Puebla or Tlaxcala, Mexico, ca. 1400–1500. Mineral and vegetable pigments on deerskin, 10 5/8″ × 10 3/8″. Biblioteca Apostolica Vaticana, Rome.

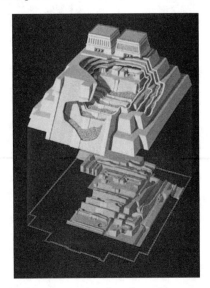

FIG. 35-03 Reconstruction drawing with cutaway view of various rebuildings of the Great Temple, Aztec, Tenochtitlán, Mexico City, Mexico, ca. 1400–1500. C = Coyolxauhqui disk (FIG. 35-4).

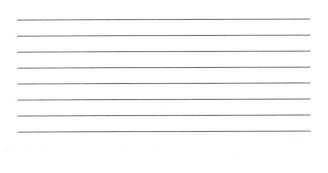

304

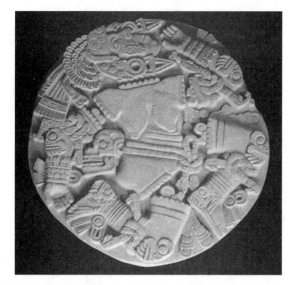

FIG. 35-04 Coyolxauhqui, from the Great Temple of Tenochtitlan, Mexico City, Mexico, Aztec, ca. 1469. Stone, diameter, 10′10″. Museo del Templo Mayor, Mexico City.

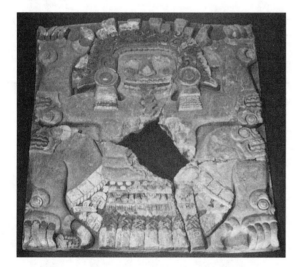

FIG. 35-05 Tlaltechuhli (Earth Lord), from the Great Temple of Tenochtitlan, mexico City, Mexico, Aztec, 1502. Andestine, painted with mineral colors, 13′9″ × 11′10 1/2″. Museo del Templo Mayor, Mexico City.

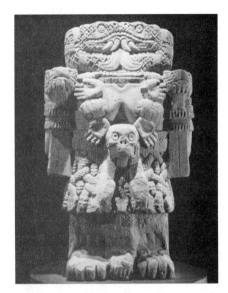

FIG. 35-06 Coatlicue from Tenochtitlan, Mexico City, Mexico, Aztec, ca. 1487–1520. Andesite, 11′ 6″ high. Museo Nacional de Antropologia, Mexico City.

_____
_____
_____
_____
_____
_____
_____
_____

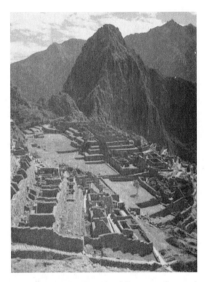

FIG. 35-07 Machu Picchu (looking northwest), Peru, Inka, 15th century.

_____
_____
_____
_____
_____
_____
_____
_____

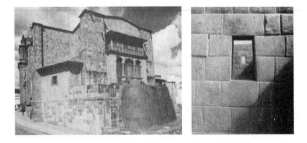

FIG. 35-08 Remains of the Temple of the Sun (surmounted by the church of Santo Domingo), Inka, Cuzco, Peru, 15th century. Exterior _(left);_ interior _(right)._

_____
_____
_____
_____
_____
_____
_____
_____

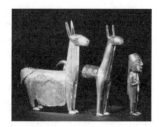

FIG. 35-08A Inka llama, alpaca, and woman, ca. 1475–1532.

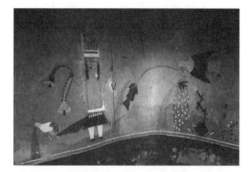

FIG. 35-09 Detail of a kiva mural from Kuaua Pueblo (Coronado State Monument), Ancestral Puebloan, New Mexico, late 15th to early 16th century. Interior of the kiva, 18′ × 18′. Museum of New Mexico, Santa Fe.

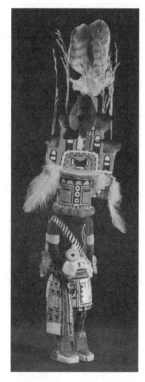

FIG. 35-10 OTTO PENTEWA, Katsina Figurine, New Oraibi, Arizona, Hopi, carved before 1959. Cottonwood root and feathers, 1′ high. Arizona State Museum, University of Arizona, Tucson.

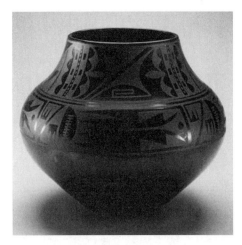

FIG. 35-11 MARÍA MONTOYA MARTÍNEZ, jar, San Ildefonso Pueblo, New Mexico, ca. 1939. Blackware, 11 1/8″ × 1′ 1″. National Museum of Women in the Arts, Washington, D.C. (gift of Wallace and Wilhelmina Hollachy).

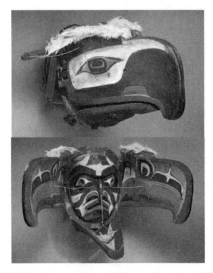

FIG. 35-12 Eagle transformation mask, closed *(top)* and open *(bottom)* views, Kwakiutl, Alert Bay, Canada, late 19th century. Wood feathers, and string, 1′ 10″ × 11″. American Museum of Natural History, New York.

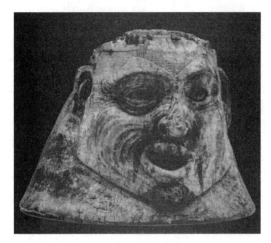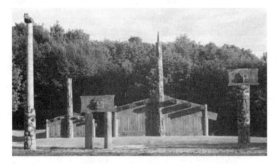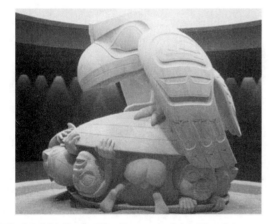

FIG. 35-13 War helmet mask, Tlingit, Canada, collected 1888–1893. Wood 1′ high. American Museum of Natural History, New York.

FIG. 35-14 BILL REID (Haida), assisted by DOUG CRANMER (Kwakiutl), reconstruction of a 19th century Haida village with totem poles, Queen Charlotte Island Canada, 1962.

FIG. 35-14A REID, The Raven and the First Men, 1978–1980.

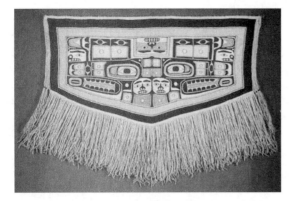

FIG. 35-15 Chilkat blanket with stylized animal motifs, Tlingit, Canada, early 20th century. Mountain goat wool and cedar bark, 2′ 11″ × 6′. Southwest Museum, Los Angeles.

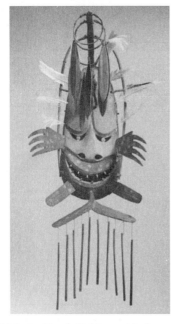

FIG. 35-16 Mask, Yupik Eskimo, Alaska, early 20th century. Wood and feathers, 3′ 9″ high. Metropolitan Museum of Art, New York (Michael C. Rockefeller Memorial Collection, gift of Nelson Rockefeller).

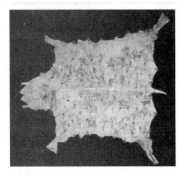

FIG. 35-16A Mandan buffalo-hide robe, ca.1800.

310

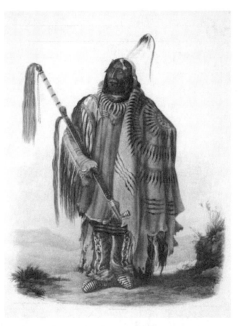

FIG. 35-17 KARL BODMER, Hidastsa Warrior Pehriska-Ruhpa (Two Ravens), Engraving by Paul Legrand after the original watercolor in the Joslyn Art Museum, Omaha, 1′3 7/8″ × 11 1/2″. Engraving; Buffalo Bill Historical Center, Cody.

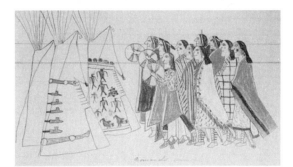

FIG. 35-18 Honoring song at painted tipi, in Julian Scott Ledger, Kiowa, 1880. Pencil, ink, and colored pencil, 7 1/2″ × 1′. Mr. and Mrs. Charles Diker Collection.

Chapter 36

Oceania

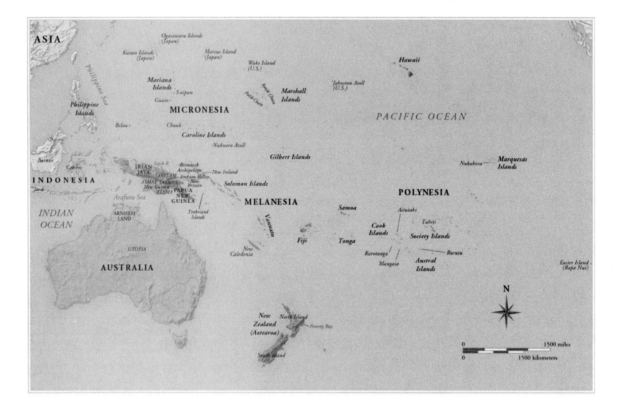

MAP 36-01 Oceania.

_____
_____
_____
_____
_____

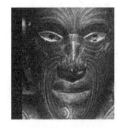

FIG. 36-01 RAHARUHI RUKUPO and Others, interior of the Te Hau-ki-Turanga meetinghouse, Poverty Bay, New Zealand, Polynesia, 1842–1845. Reconstructed in the National Museum of New Zealand, Wellington.

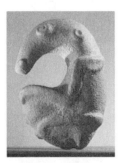

FIG. 36-01A Ambum Stone, Papua New Guinea, ca. 1500 BCE.

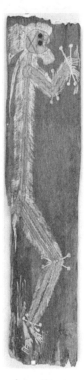

FIG. 36-02 Auuenau, from Western Arnhem Land Australia, 1913. Ochre on bark, 4′ 10 2/3″ × 1′ 1″. South, Australian Museum, Adelaide.

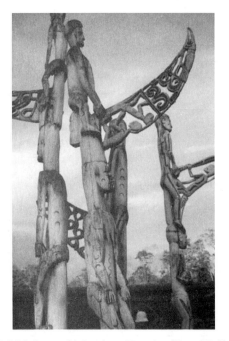

FIG. 36-03 Asmat bisj pokes, Buepis village, Fajit River, Casuarina Coast, Irian Jaya, Melanesia, early to mid 20th century.

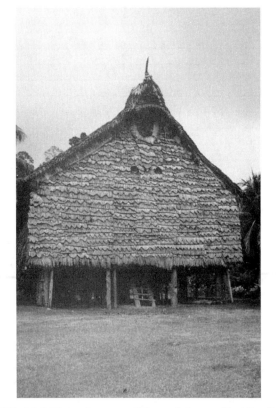

FIG. 36-04 Iatmul ceremonial men's house, East Sepik, Papua New Guinea, Melanesia, mid-to late 20th century.

314

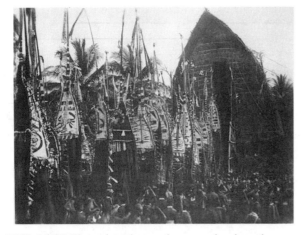

FIG. 36-05 Elema hevehe masks retreating into the men's house, Orokolo Bay, Papua New Guinea, Melanesia, early to mid-20th century.

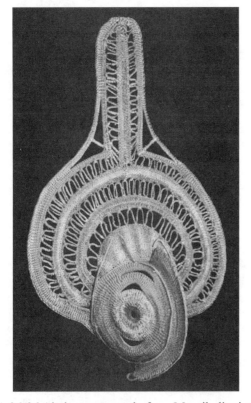

FIG. 36-06 Abelam yam mask, from Maprik district, Papua New Guinea, Melanesia. Painted cane, 1′ 6 9/10″ high. Musée Barbier-Mueller, Geneva.

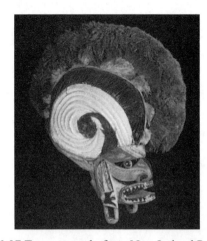

FIG. 36-07 Tatanua mask, from New Ireland Papua
New Guinea, Melanesia, 19th to 20th centuries. Wood
fiber, shell, lime, and feathers, 1′ 5 1/2″ high. Otago
Museum, Dunedin.

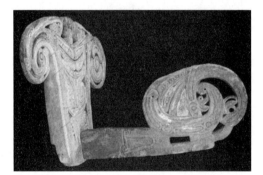

FIG. 36-08 Canoe prow and splashboard, from
Trobriand Islands, Papua New Guinea, Melanesia,
19th to 20th centuries. Wood and paint, 1′ 3 1/2″ high,
1′ 11″ long. Musée du quai Branly, Paris.

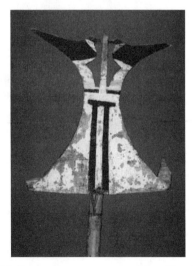

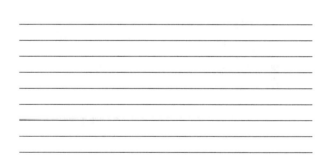

FIG. 36-09 Canoe prow ornament, from Chunk,
Caroline Islands, late 19th century. Painted wood birds
11″ × 10 5/8″. British Museum, London.

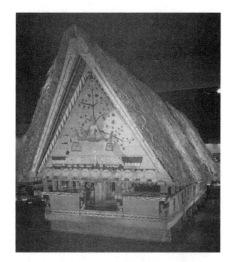

FIG. 36-10 Men's ceremonial house, from Belau (Palau), Republic of Belau, Micronesia, 20th century. Ethnologisches Museum, Staatliche Museen zu Berlin, Berlin.

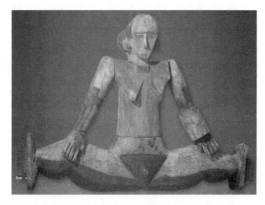

FIG. 36-11 Dilukai, from Belau (Palau). Wood, pigment, and fiber, 1′11 5/8″ high. Linden Museum, Stuttgart.

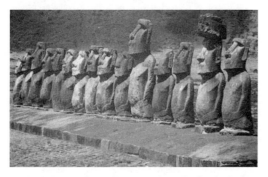

FIG. 36-12 Row of moai on a stone platform, Rapa Nui (Easter Island), Polynesia, 10th to 12th centuries. Volcanic tuff and red scoria. Tallest statue approximately 19′ high.

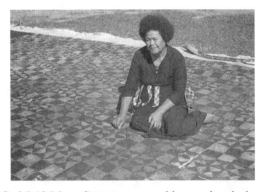

FIG. 36-13 MELE SITANI, ngatu with manulua designs, Tonga, Polynesia, 1967. Barkcloth.

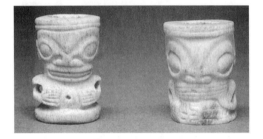

FIG. 36-14 Hair ornaments from the Marquesas Islands, Polynesia, collected in the 1870s. Bone, 1 1/2″ high *(left)*, 1 2/5″ high *(right)*. University of Pennsylvania Museum of Archaeology and Anthropology, Philadelphia.

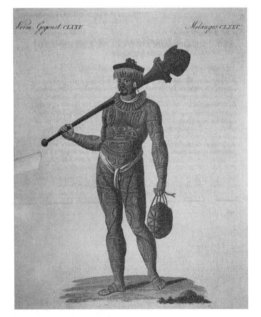

FIG. 36-15 Tattooed warrior with war club, Nukahiva, Marquesas Islands, Polynesia, early 19th century. Color engraving in Carl Bertuch, *Bilderbuch für Kinder* (Weimar, 1813). (page 883)

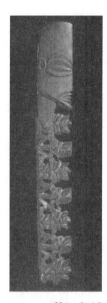

FIG. 36-15A Rarotonga staff god, 19th or early 20th century.

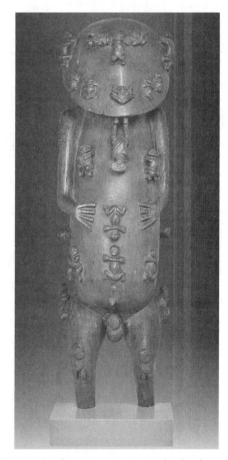

FIG. 36-16 A'a, from Rurutu, Austral Islands, Polynesia, late 18th or early 19th century. Wood, 3′8″high. British Museum, London.

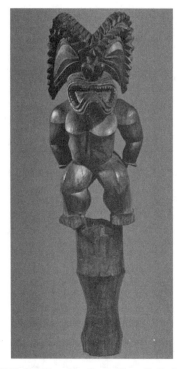

FIG. 36-17 Kuka'ilimoku, from Hawaii, Polynesia, late 18th or early 19th century. Wood, 2′ 5 3/4″ high (figure only). British Museum, London.

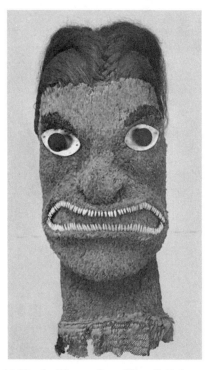

FIG 36-18 Head of Lono, from Hawaii, Polynesia, ca. 1775–1780. Feathers over wicker work, human hair, dog's teeth, and pearl shells, 2′ 3/4″ high. British Museum, London. (page 884)

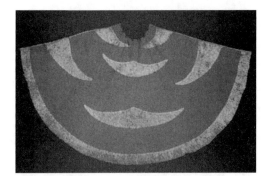

FIG 36-19 Feather cloak, from Hawaii, Polynesia, ca. 1824–1843. Feathers and fiber netting, 4/8 1/3″ × 8′. Bishop Pauahi Museum, Honolulu.

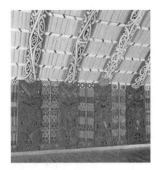

FIG 36-19A Mataatua meetinghouse, Maori, 1871–1875.

Chapter 37

Africa: 1800 to 1980

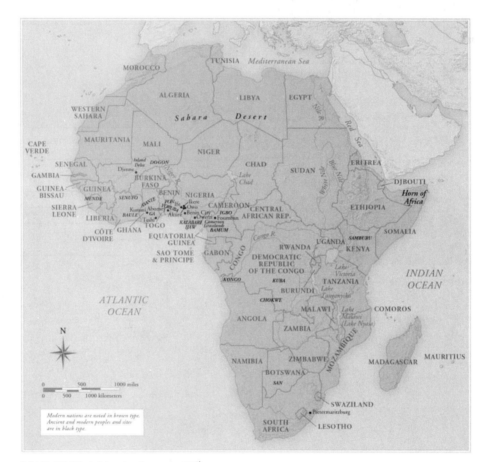

MAP 37-01 Africa in the early 21ˢᵗ century.

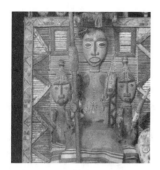

FIG. 37-01 Ancestral screen (nduen fobara), Kalabari
Ijaw, Nigeria, late 19th century. Wood, fiber, and cloth,
3′ 9 1/2″ high. British Museum, London.

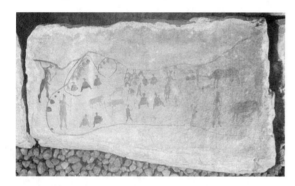

FIG. 37-02 Stock raid with cattle, horses, encampment,
rock painting, San, from Bamboo Mountain, South
Africa, mid 19th century. Natal Museum,
Pietermaritzburg.

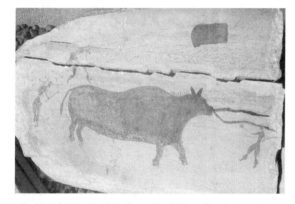

FIG. 37-03 Magical "rain animal," rockpainting, San,
from Bamboo Mountains, South Africa, mid 19th
century, Natal Museum, Pietermaritzburg.

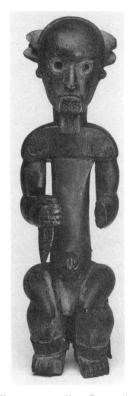

FIG. 37-04 Reliquary guardian figure (bieri), Fang, Gabon, late 19th century. Wood 1′ 8 3/8″ high. Philadelphia, Museum of Art, Philadelphia.

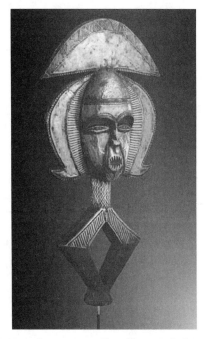

FIG. 37-05 Reliquary guardian figure (mbulu ngulu), Kota, Gabon, 19th or early 20th century. Wood, copper, iron, and brass, 1′ 9 1/16″ high. Musée Barbier-Mueller, Geneva.

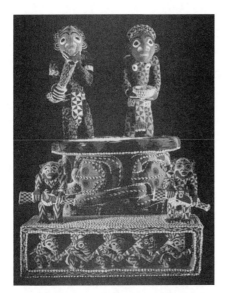

FIG. 37-06 Throne and footstool of King Nsangu, Bamum, Cameroon, ca. 1870. Wood textile, glass beads, and cowrie shells, 5′ 9″ high. Museum für Völkerkunde, Staatliche Museen zu Berlin, Berlin.

_____
_____
_____
_____
_____
_____
_____
_____
_____

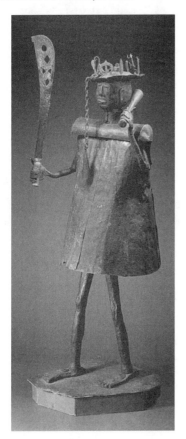

FIG. 37-07 AKATI AKPELE KENDO, Warrior figure (Gu?), from the palace of King Glele, Abomey, Fon, Republic of Benin, 1858–1859. Iron, 5′ 5″ high. Musée du quai Branly, Paris.

_____
_____
_____
_____
_____
_____
_____
_____
_____

325

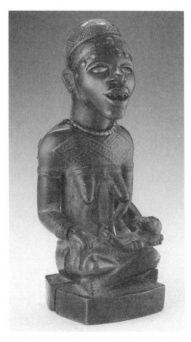

FIG. 37-08 Yombe mother and child (pfemba), Kongo, Democratic Republic of Congo, late 19th century. Wood glass, glass beads, brass tacks, and pigment, 10 1/8″ high. National Museum of African Art, Washington, D.C.

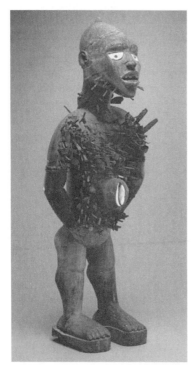

FIG. 37-09 Nail figure (nkisi n'kondi), Kongo, from Shiloango River area, Democratic Republic of Congo, ca. 1875–1900. Wood nails, blades, medicinal materials, and cowrie shell, 3′ 10 3/4″ high. Detroit Institute of Arts, Detroit.

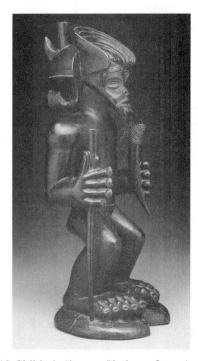

FIG 34-10 Chibinda Ilunga, Chokwe, from Angola or Democratic Republic of Congo, late 19th to 20th century. Wood and human hair, 1′ 4″ high. Kimbell Art Museum, Fort Worth.

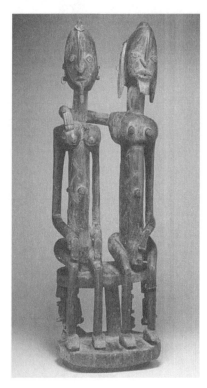

FIG. 37-11 Seated couple, Dogon, Mali, ca. 1800–1850. Wood, 2′ 4″ high. Metropolitan Museum of Art, New York (gift of Lester Wunderman).

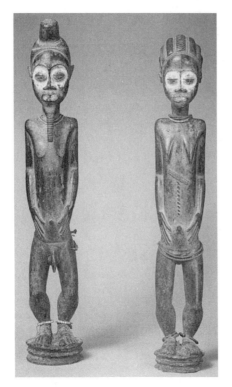

FIG. 37-12 Male and female figures, probably bush spirits (asye usu), Baule, Côte d'Ivoire, late 19th or early 20th century. Wood beads, and kaolin, man 1′ 9 3/4″ high, woman 1′ 8 5/8″ high. Metropolitan Museum of Art, New York, (Michael C. Rockefeller Memorial Collection, gift of Nelson A. Rockefeller).

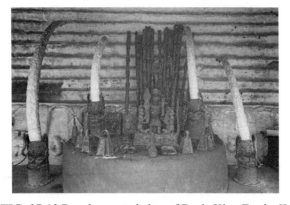

FIG. 37-13 Royal ancestral altar of Benin King Eweka II, in the palace in Benin City, Nigeria, photographed in 1970. Clay, copper alloy, wood and ivory.

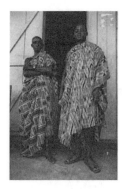

FIG. 37-13A Asante noblemen in kente cloth robes, 1972.

_____
_____
_____
_____
_____
_____
_____
_____
_____
_____

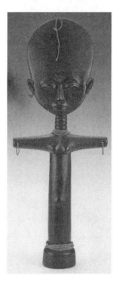

FIG. 37-14 Osei Bonsu, Akua'ba (Akua's child), Asante, Ghana, ca. 1935. Wood, beads, and pigment, 10 1/4″ high. Private collection.

_____
_____
_____
_____
_____
_____
_____
_____
_____
_____

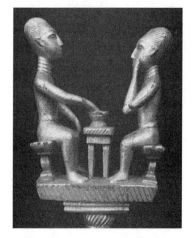

FIG. 37-15 Osei Bonsu, linguist's staff of two men sitting at a table of food Asante, Ghana, mid-20th century. Wood and gold leaf, section shown 10″ high. Collection of the Paramount Chief of Offinso, Asante.

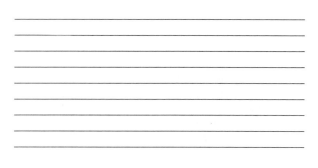

_____
_____
_____
_____
_____
_____
_____
_____
_____

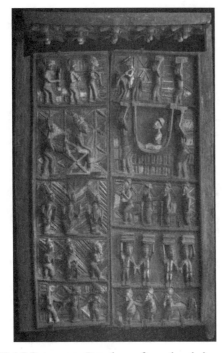

FIG 37-16 OLOWE OF ISE, doors from the shrine of the king's head Ikere, Yoruba, Nigeria, 1910–1914. Painted wood 6' high. British Museum, London.

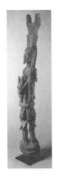

FIG. 37-16A OLOWE OF ISE, veranda post, Akure, 1920s.

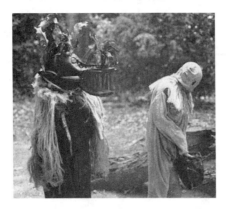

FIG. 37-17 Senufo masquerader, Côte d'Ivoire, photographed ca. 1980–1990.

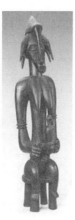

FIG. 37-17A Ancient Mother, Senufo, early
20th century.

_____
_____
_____
_____
_____
_____
_____
_____
_____
_____

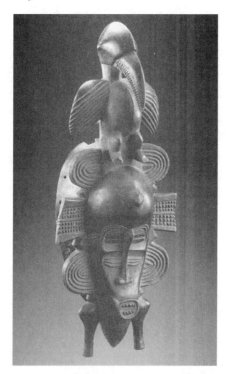

FIG. 37-18 "Beautiful Lady" dance mask, Senufo,
Côte d'Ivoire, late 20th century. Wood 1′ 1/2″ high.
Musée Barbier-Mueller, Geneva.

_____
_____
_____
_____
_____
_____
_____
_____
_____

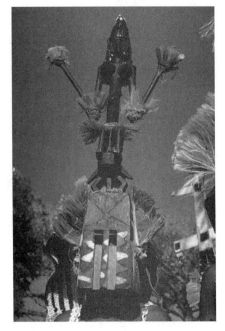

FIG. 37-19 Satimbe masquerader, Dogon, Mali, mid-to late 20th century.

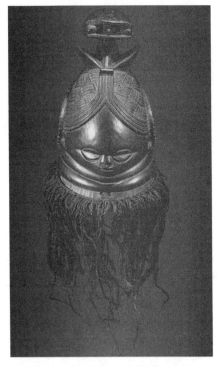

FIG. 37-20 Female mask, Mende, Sierra Leone, 20th century. Wood and pigment, 1′ 2 1/2″ high. Fowler Museum of Cultural History, University of California, Los Angeles (gift of the Wellcome Trust).

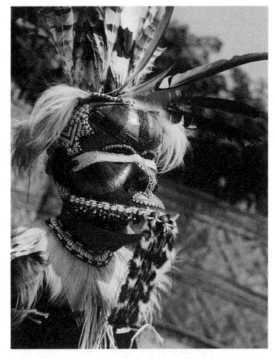

FIG. 37-21 Bwoom masquerader, Kuba, Democratic
Republic of Congo, photographed ca. 1950.

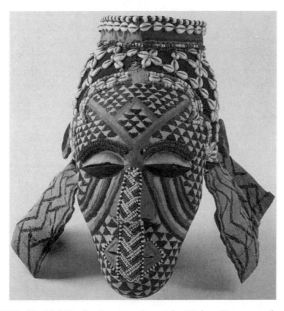

FIG. 37-22 Ngady Amwaash mask, Kuba, Democratic
Republic of Congo, late 19th or early 20th century.
Peabody Museum, Harvard University, Cambridge.

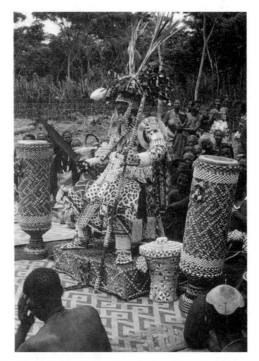

FIG. 37-23 Kuba King Kot a-Mbweeky III during a display for photographer and filmmaker Eliot Elisofon in 1970, Mushenge, Democratic Republic of Congo.

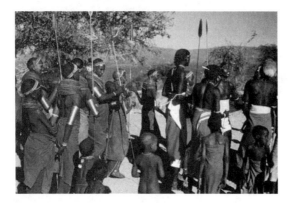

FIG. 37-24 Samburu men and women dancing, northern Kenya, photographed in 1973.

334

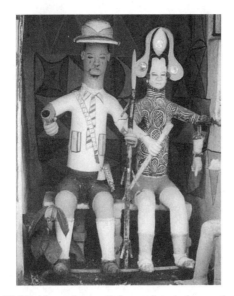

FIG. 37-25 Ala and Amadioha, painted clay sculptures in an mbari, Igbo, Umugote Orishaeze, Nigeria, photographed in 1966.

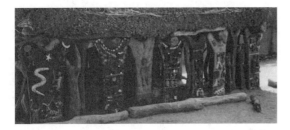

FIG. 37-26 Togu na (men's house of words), Dogon, Mali, photographed in 1989.